MW01098321

River of Dreams

River of Dreams

Lani Waller

Illustrations by Bill Allan

West River Publishing

Published by
West River Publishing
P.O. Box 15
Grand Island, NY 14072

Printed in the United States of America

First edition

10 9 8 7 6 5 4 3 2 1

Cataloging-in-Publication Data is available on file.

ISBN 0-9633109-3-3

to Judy

Contents

Foreword

I first received a story on fly-fishing from Lani Waller in late 1978, on the fabulous rainbow trout fishing to be found in the Katmai Monument on the Alaskan Peninsula. It was a revelation to me, both as a fly fisher and as a magazine editor. I had never visited Alaska and as a resident of the "Lower 48," I had the usual preconception of that place as full of glaciers, bears, and salmon. A first read of his manuscript changed me, lifted me, and within twelve months I was floating the Alagnak River and absorbing the unspoiled wilderness fishing that Waller had sketched in his piece ("Alaska's Katmai Rainbows", *Fly Fisherman* Magazine, Spring Special 1979).

Lani's piece inspired our subsequent magazine section "Great Waters: Alaska" and the fly-fishing lodge industry in Alaska received a shot of adrenaline that continues to this day, despite a recent stumble due to the 9/11 event that terrified airline travelers.

Why did Waller's piece hit such a nerve among the fly fishers of the world? Quite simply because his exceptional writing style evoked the same response in them that it had in me. Waller saw and described Alaskan fly-fishing through the spiritual eyes of a true fly fisher. He is one of those rare writers who walks the walk and writes the walk, speaking to those who live a life of fly-fishing and cherish its special values.

Let's be honest. By publicizing the unspoiled places, we inadvertently sully the very thing we love most—their rare, untrammeled, lonely, natural beauty. A whole industry was created by the seminal pieces written on Alaska's fabulous fly-fishing wilderness. And Waller, stunned by the ensuing publicity, eventually retreated from writing pieces on his first loves, the places where wild fish still hold in unspoiled waters, and for the most part, he quit writing, and moved on to new frontiers, including inshore and offshore salt water, and the hidden places of the angler's emotional perspective.

But that is all biographical history presented here simply to sketch his values. Well, I lost a superb writer and kept a great friend, someone with whom I shared many important values.

I thought about it for a long time—about two decades. Then, one day, I sat him down and said: "Listen, you have to write a book. You must leave something of yourself. You write too well not to leave a bequest to the rest of us. You have something to say and there is a peculiar thing about our sport and its literature: the personal voices are the truly important elements of our value system. We will soon lose an entire generation of fly fishing writers. Your voice must be part of the footprint that we leave for the next generation."

He wrote this, his first book, and re-wrote it under the advice of the best book editors, and got into the groove and that's what we have here.

And what do we have? The best of Waller, the soul of the man, a personal statement written in the easy style that only Waller has. No frills: a personal journey, the story of a 60's Generation West Coast free spirit who wandered here and there to find himself and finally did so on the waters where wild fish are making their last stand. In the process he became a true conservationist, a leader in the fight to save some of nature's most beautiful and fragile creatures.

Foreword

The great fly fishing books keep coming and going and they are all personal testimonies—and this is one of them, a must read for true fly fishers. Lani Waller is the spiritual leader of this band of brothers. His voice is the rally call to those of us who know that the industrial juggernaut that stalks our remaining wilderness must be controlled or we will lose our sport and sooner or later, our soul. If we lose these things, there will be no more Lani Wallers or the literature of values they might create.

Last September 13th I was sitting beside a steelhead pool in British Columbia. The river had been in and out due to the autumnal monsoons and I was tired from wading and casting, casting and wading into milky water. Then the sun came out to dry me and it lit the valley like new hope. I rose and addressed the pool, working carefully down toward the tail. With each presentation my heart was in my mouth. I simply knew it would happen. The line stopped hard, then throbbed violently. A large silver bullet shot from the pool, then ran leaping across the pool in a shower of silvery spray. Five minutes later I had the hen steelhead at my feet.

I held her there, quivering on the sand and examined her. Her eye was wild, her sides sleek and white, her back black. I held her gently in the flow. Suddenly she shot away. Part of me went with her, the part that Lani Waller had helped to create. I am a brother in Waller's army, those spiritual brothers who know and live with the remaining wild places of the world.

John Randolph
Harrisburg, Pennsylvania
April, 2004

Introduction

Each person we meet has a particular uniqueness, and I believe that we are each a reflection or product of the sum of our life's best and worst experiences. I'm sure we've all wondered how much of the best of our lives we might have missed if a certain parent, spouse, child, teacher, friend or pet had not been there for us. Lani Waller has been one of those wonderful influences that has touched my life, adding his special portion and making me a better person for the experiences we've shared. He is also a perfect example of why a person is what he is, their lives being rich with an amazing variety of people and experiences.

When Lani asked me to review his *River of Dreams* and write a part of the foreword, I felt it was an honor, and one that I'll always treasure. I found that with each story I read, I wanted to go back and slowly read it again to appreciate the amazing depth and perspective he gives us while sharing some of his most meaningful experiences.

My life came together with Lani's so uniquely that it's almost a story in itself. It all began one glorious week in October some years ago, when I discovered the Babine River and its magnificent strain of steelhead. I was so moved by my experience that I wanted to help preserve these incredible fish and I wrote an article in *Outdoor Life* about the Babine to encourage no-kill regulations. Happily this did eventually happen.

Several years later, Scientific Anglers\3M Company sent me a video they had produced on catching trophy steelhead. The soft-spoken young man in the video was Lani Waller, and right then and there Lani began inspiring me to be a better steelheader (and human being). Lani was my steelhead role model and hero.

The next steelhead season after the release of the videos I returned to the Babine and happened to see Lani at the Smithers Airport, but I missed the opportunity to meet him. Another year passed and I was at a fly fishing expo in Seattle when Lani and I passed in a narrow hotel hallway, making brief eye contact. We both walked on several steps and then turned around, at the same time, and spoke each other's name. Right then we both felt a strong connection with each other and in the following moments expressed our appreciation for each other's work.

What Lani told me blew my mind. My Babine article had actually influenced him to travel to the Babine and become a life-long devotee of the river and to help preserve its incredible steelhead. Our friendship quickly grew, with a real highlight being the opportunity for my wife Emily and me to spend a week with Lani on the Babine at Chick Stewart's camp. That week with Lani and Emily was one of those profound experiences that changes you, and adds to your life. Lani's way of teaching us to catch those magnificent steelhead showed respect for these great fish and this one-of-a-kind river, and ways to get so much more from the total experience. How fortunate the three of us were and we left with a deep and abiding friendship, one which continues to this day.

After finishing Lani's manuscript I know that you will read this book many more times. Each time Emily and I have, it has made us smile, laugh, and cry. In "River of Dreams" Lani has connected all his life's dots—family, wife, friends, pets, fishing, and the greatest joys and the most heartbreaking moments—in a truly remarkable series of stories.

At one point in his life, when Lani was fighting for his life after a devastating plane crash, I remember telling him that if he didn't give up, the very best of his life was still ahead of him. He didn't give up and this book is proof that a man like Lani is the sum of his life's experiences and that life's best years are yet to come if we persist.

It's my suggestion, to get the most out of this good read, that you turn off your cell phone, find some quiet place where you can relax without distraction and savor each sentence of this book as if it were a rare bite of gourmet food ... nourishment for the heart, soul and mind.

Thanks Lani for making our lives better with yours.

Dave Whitlock
Midway, Arkansas
May, 2004

Author's Notes

I find it interesting that so much has been said and written about why we say and write so much about fishing. As Montana angler and author Tom McGuane has pointed out, the endeavor is uniquely and powerfully personal, with a human intimacy which seems to inspire expression, if not at times, demand it. He's right. There is something here and it resonates to the core. I would find it more perplexing if less were said.

Season by season, my own perspective has developed. Like so many others, I started with the literature about the Neversink and the Madison, the romanticism of ancient brook trout, the dusty books about wet flies and streamers, the old wooden rods and gut leaders, and so on. But I didn't, and in fact couldn't, stay there. Eventually I found myself standing somewhere on the edge of a world in which the ordinary history, technical facts and physical science of fishing were not enough to carry me to full term.

At times my addiction to the sport has exceeded all normal bounds. I used to fiberglass my fly-fishing skiffs in my living room. The occasional spill would require cleaning the rug with a hammer. The guy in the brown suit I met at a cocktail party looked like a mullet. I'm sure he was a fine gentleman, but in my mind the angling perspective had become the measure of all, and the word mullet seemed to define, perfectly, his countenance. In the dental chair I discovered my orthodontist was "one of us," and suddenly my root canal was no longer a surgical process but a passionate discussion of the virtues of steelhead versus Atlantic salmon.

In later years, perhaps because of advancing age and approaching mortality, the boundaries between life and fishing seem to be blurring. Fisheries conservation, political struggles with the good old boys who want to cut all the trees and net all the salmon, and First Nations land claims against the British Columbia government have somehow become inseparable from leaders, roll casts and recreation, including tickets for the next flight to the Bahamas, or, for that matter, a rock concert in Las Vegas and the red gill plates of a Mexican dorado.

I've had the best of help along the way. Michael Fong, whom I miss dearly, gave me my first writing assignment in 1976, something I will never forget. Not long thereafter, John Randolph, Editor and Publisher of *Fly Fisherman* magazine, gave me an editorial position on the magazine and he has remained a constant friend, and confidant. Mel and Fanny Krieger added a measure of friendship and a dialogue that has gone on now for twenty-seven years—one that went well beyond the badly needed casting instruction.

Tom Pero, editor of *Wild Steelhead and Salmon* and now *Fish & Fly* magazine helped immensely by publishing the first "non-technical" piece I ever wrote, and a letter I received from steelhead angler and writer Bill McMillan about that piece made all the difference. The remarks of painter and friend Bill Allan and angling authors Seth Norman, Trey Combs and Dave Whitlock all were of vital help. Filmmaker Jeffrey Pill helped at a critical time and as did mentor Laurance Kaplan. In recent seasons Nick Lyons, Scott Ferguson, Russell Chatham and Chris Santella helped provide focus. Rick and Jerry Kustich have been of constant help from the beginning. Ken Morrish and Brian Gies of Fly Water Travel deserve a plug for recent expansion of The Dream and now I go anywhere they say I should.

Author's Notes

As far as this manuscript is concerned, one person stood above all others and without his patient help anything could have happened. Chapter Three, for example, might have included information on the chemical composition of the wax used to shine the floor of the New York Stock Exchange. Chapter Seven could have wandered into Africa with a description of the left wing structure of the African tse-tse fly, and Chapter Nine might have included a description of the time I slipped while winter steelhead fishing and fell into the latrine at the campground on the Navarro River. Steve Raymond was essential and helped teach me the difference between censorship and editing, and in the process illuminated many of the responsibilities of written communication.

Steve also told me that what I ended up with placed a certain responsibility, perhaps even a burden, upon the reader. Four of the chapters, he reminded me, are about death. Many of the others soon wander from fishing and descend into the realm of what Chatham has referred to as "the deeply eccentric." My only response is this: it is personal archeology. The explorations seemed inevitable and somehow necessary.

If I were to do this all over, I am quite sure that in many instances I would describe the descent differently. I have decided, however to leave it as you see it here and move on to the next dig.

What you read here won't teach you how to catch more fish on your trip to the Adirondacks, Lake Iliamna, Ascension Bay or the Sustut River in northern British Columbia. The stories and essays here represent my attempts to illuminate something else—the place of personal values, perceptions, and the private things that over the years have seemed an essential part of my marriage to fishing.

In the past dozen seasons or so, I have come to realize that the best of angling comes as much from the minds and casts of others as from anything I might think or do. That's true, somehow, even of people who don't fish—and especially true when I consider the woman I ended up marrying. We had dinner one night, long ago, with my eight foot skiff, the "Oasis," still sitting in the living room.

One of the mixing pans had bonded to the floor and I was indeed using a hammer to clean the carpet. The work was nearly finished and we sat in the boat that night with a few cans of cleaning solvent, a roll of silver glass cloth, some red wine and a pizza.

When the pram was finished, I took Judy for a cruise in the estuary off Larkspur, California, to show her a couple of my favorite haunts for striped bass. At one point a luxury craft passed and the folks partying on the rear deck looked down at us with a curiosity apparently saturated with booze, and their particular sense of social values. One of them raised a glass, and they all passed into oblivion drinking champagne. I looked at Judy. She smiled and said I had a nice boat. When we returned to shore I proposed and she said "yes," in the tall reeds and tidal marshes where I had often cast to schools of feeding bass.

That was almost thirty years ago. In that time I have rowed, motored and flown over a great deal of the planet with her and some of the best people in the world in search of perfect fishing and the best possible life. With few exceptions it has been a marvelous journey. The explanations and perspectives included here, both personal and social, are my own and I take full responsibility for them, but they would be nothing without her and those I have known and traveled with.

Thanks to all.

Lani Waller
Novato, California
September, 2002

Trotter's Pool

What you are about to read actually happened. After that September day, nothing would be the same. Including the sport of angling. The events of that day became a lens—one which not only re-focused my past experiences as an angler, but one which re-defined the future—and an odyssey too real to ignore or escape. In the end, the story now in front of you was really written by four men. I am merely standing in for the other three.

~

Upriver, two pools away from the cabins, a secondary tributary comes in from the mountains carrying a touch of blue glacial ice. It hits the main river hard, turning right, then left before settling into a pool of water perfect in form but chilled from the thawing of frozen snows some interminable distance to the north.

The forest along the river where I now stand rises to the sky with trees so tall you must strain your neck to see their tops. The trees are rooted in river rock and red earth, and eagles or ravens often rest in the limbs. The canopy of spruce, hemlock and cottonwood seems impenetrable and their shadows spread over the tannic stain of the Babine River in northern British Columbia like an umbrella.

Steelhead can be almost anywhere. They come to the fly hard, without warning, lifting themselves up through shafts of yellow sunlight, exploding in quicksilver bursts. They are indeed beautiful.

Two anglers are fishing the pool, one behind the other, separated by at least a hundred yards of river. Waist-deep in heavy current, the upstream fisherman is framed in mist and the heavy chop of incoming rapids. His line is a long one and his companion pauses for a moment to watch in appreciation as it reaches out, penetrating the shadows and falling perfectly to the surface.

The downstream angler has another great angling passion besides Canadian steelhead: he also loves fishing for saltwater permit in Central America. He likes to talk about both species and does so rabidly. He speaks with genuine authority.

"I'm here to help you, Waller," he has told me, "because, God knows, you can use the help."

Today is the last day of a seven-day odyssey and return to the river on the exact anniversary of what I now simply call "The Accident." The rod in my hands is made from long splinters of bamboo, shaped carefully and glued together. It represents three weeks of a man's life. It was a gift, a thoughtful gesture from a friend to help me heal from endless injections, rubber tubes, countless nightmares, a crushed face, ruptured eye and other injuries, both physical and mental. I accepted it with greater feelings than I could express, looking away so that others could not see my tears.

A reel was added to the rod, another gift, hand-built by Dave McNeese, beautiful and smooth with graceful curling handles and a drag as smooth as silk, as they say.

Now, on this September day, there is not much time left to fish. It's our last day, and most of the stuff we brought with us for the week's fishing is already packed away. It's time to go home.

The rest of our party has decided to wait in camp for the helicopter that will take us all back to town, to the world most steelheaders merely tolerate between fishing trips. Only Will and I remain in the cold water.

Trotter's Pool

We fish differently and yet each of us understands the private dreams of the other. If it weren't so deadly, I could almost detest his favorite steelhead fly: a ten-inch strip of black rabbit fur that crawls through the water like a wounded snake. He in turn regards my dry flies with horror; his southern Missouri drawl slips through his tobacco-stained mustache with obscene jokes about the sexual preferences of anyone who would use flies like those "Gawdamn things."

For the past six days our plan has been simple: pound the hell out of the river until you catch a fish. The first part of it has been easy enough, but the second has sometimes been a little more difficult. Only two fish of any size have been taken. Another friend, "Popsicle" Reynolds, has landed a steelhead of about twenty pounds, his first on the fly. Could be beginner's luck. Most likely he owes his success to the fact that he fishes like a demon; neither he nor his hot pink puff of marabou will come out of the water until the sky loses all color and the river around his waist is black.

Will landed the other big fish, one perhaps even larger than twenty pounds. He took it in a pool called the Triple Header, and I cringed through the camera lens at the sight of the bulky, heavy-shouldered male with the ten-inch strip of fur dangling from its lip, looking much like one of its captor's cigarettes.

Someone—Lee Wulff, I think it was—once said the fly is a dream sent down with faith and hope attached to it, to a world the angler can love but never understand. I don't know if this sentiment included monstrous strips of fur lashed to a hook with black shoemaker's twine and purple strips of plastic. It probably did.

It has been raining for almost two days. The river is now in that indeterminate state somewhere between absolutely hopeless slate-gray and "maybe-it's-clearing-a-little" dirty green. Below me, where the lower end of the pool loosens up a little from the choke of heavy water coming in above, an invisible pod of steelhead often holds in a pocket just below a faint crease in the center of the stream. There is time, perhaps, for one more cast to the spot.

The last cast, on the last pool, is sometimes a sad thing, because rivers have a way of leaving you sooner or later. To let go is not easy, perhaps because one of the things that always accompanies the last cast is a faraway feeling that whispers about the end of your fishing, and waters that will one day move only in the mind.

But the cast is a good one. Translucent and beautiful, the line rolls through the air, shining in the gray light and singing through silver guides and yellow Chinese wood. It drops into a rolling fog of water.

Now the line is in shadow, thick in the middle with a thin tip and a crystal leader that drags the half-swimming, half-sunk fly toward the crease where the steelhead usually hold. It drifts downstream in a wash of dirty gray water.

A light pluck is felt on the line, almost imperceptible, so delicate it seems thin and dreamlike. Then comes another. And a third.

Then nothing.

Suddenly the line tightens and surges forward, pulling the rod down in a series of lunges that stretch the line as tight as piano wire. There is a hydraulic lift of foam and swirling water, then the fish turns and rushes downstream into a reach of white water more than a hundred yards long.

An hour later and a mile downstream, almost back to the cluster of cabins, the steelhead lifts itself for the last time in the amber water. Like a red and silver zeppelin suspended on a nylon leash, it comes finally to the yellow rod and the two anglers waiting patiently on shore.

"How big is it, Will? Can you see it yet?"

"Yeah, yeah . . . I can see it. It ain't that long, but it's pretty fat."

The obedient zeppelin arrives with fins extended like erect, translucent wings. Its back is the color of cold gray steel and a slash of red runs all the way down its sides. Will smiles, kneels next to the fish and stretches a length of plastic tape along its flanks.

"Thirty-eight-by-nineteen," he says. "Maybe a little more." Then, after a pause: "About twenty pounds. Not bad for one of those gawdamn flies you think are so good." He spits in the water.

"Cigarette?"

"OK, thanks."

"I love you, you bastard."

"Yeah, yeah, I know. I love you too."

Overhead the sky seems stretched tightly between parallel rows of tall, dark green trees. Somewhere a crow cries out and the coarse sound rolls through the woods, cracking through the air, finally dying in the cool wind.

"Do you know where we are?" Will asks.

"Yeah, I know. This is the place where the plane went down."

"Are you all right?"

"Yes."

"Well, let go of it then. It's time to leave."

"I know."

The steelhead is released and merges with the river, gone forever in a bright swirling curl. It leaves a hollow mark in the sand next to the deep imprint of a bear's paw. The print is filled with a thin purple film of water like a mirror holding the reflection of time. In it I can see three helpless forms turning slowly in the river, suspended like embryos in a cold broth of dirty water. They are without color, floating in time. They are also far away from me, already in the hands of God.

Two are friends. The third is the young pilot who brought us to the river. We had boarded the Cessna 206 on a hopeful September morning in Smithers, B.C. First was an old friend of mine, an expert Klamath River steelheader, who shook the pilot's hand and asked if he might have the co-pilot's seat. The pilot nodded and my friend climbed in and buckled up.

The second fisherman, whom I had met only the day before on the flight from Vancouver, slipped into the back seat on the right. I followed and took the seat behind the pilot. The door snapped shut;

the chrome door handle revolved and clicked into place. Seat belts were drawn tight and fastened.

We taxied onto the runway, pivoted into the breeze, rolled forward and were airborne. The town of Smithers fell behind like a collection of toys, soon replaced by geometrical farm plots that gave way in turn to ugly scars of clear-cut forests crisscrossed by too many logging roads. Eventually these too fell behind and we flew above a splendid landscape of soaring peaks and untouched timber. The view was fantastic.

The pilot and my Klamath friend talked about elevation, wind speed, headings and other things beyond my comprehension, while my back-seat companion asked about the fishing ahead of us. He wanted to know if the steelhead would be rising to a dry fly. Of course they will, I told him.

Our heading was almost due north and we were closing in on the best piece of wilderness steelhead water I have seen in forty years of searching. The tension and excitement in the Cessna cabin were almost palpable.

It was almost 9:30 a.m. when the pilot extracted a sheaf of papers from the side panel of his door and unfolded a navigational chart. He seemed nervous, and unsure of himself. How could that be I thought. Looking out the window, he manipulated the chart, rotated his vision from left to right and then, as if to assure himself, pointed left to a collection of rocky peaks that resembled the vertebrae of a giant fossilized Tyrannosaurus Rex. He put the map away as we passed quickly between the serrated stone teeth and crumbling shale cartilage of the great beast. No one said anything; the motor droned in our ears.

At 9:40 a.m. I saw something else on the left: a speck that appeared to be floating in the air like an insect. Soon wings emerged from an aluminum thorax and I recognized it was an earlier charter returning to Smithers from the Babine, having delivered four other anglers to the lodge just thirty minutes before. My headset was on and I could hear the pilot's voice crackling through the static, telling our captain that all was well. Don't be nervous he told our pilot. Take it easy. Everything is OK. Of course it's OK I thought. What could be wrong? What's he talking about?

Just ahead of us was the last yellow ridge of aspen and cottonwood that separated us from the river. I remember thinking how good everything looked.

The Babine was visible seconds later, a serpentine coil of light and current twisting into secret pools that I knew by heart and eye. I thought of the fish I had landed in these pools and others I had hooked and lost, especially one silver female that turned the water to diamonds as she struck the surface in the bright throat of a pool named Eagle before disappearing among the stones and refracted light.

No problem, I thought. We have six days ahead of us. There will be more.

We turned for the final approach. The river was fifty yards below; it looked in perfect shape. As the plane skimmed over it, my imagination dropped a dry fly into a good-looking pocket I didn't think I'd fished before. I wondered why.

The lobster-red roofs of the lodge were bright in the morning light as we descended toward the landing strip. All seemed well—and then, suddenly, without even a second's warning, the flight, the landing and everything else went to hell so fast my mind couldn't grasp what was happening. It was like a chain of falling dominoes; once the first went down all the others were fated to follow, and there was nothing I could do but watch.

We had approached from the wrong direction, touched down too late and were going too fast, with a tailwind at our backs. Somehow the flaps were in the wrong position as we tried to pull up again. Green brush at the end of the runway passed just below our wingtips, bowing in the wind. The river came next, looming up so slowly that we seemed to be hovering over it. I could see the large stone marker of Trotters Pool, curling the water just above the tailout, one of my favorite spots. We almost scraped the rock with our landing gear; too close.

Now what? I asked myself. The pilot stiffened in his seat and leaned forward, pushing the throttle and looking right and left; we gained some air speed and a little altitude, but it was too late. Fifty yards ahead and coming up at almost eighty miles an hour was a heavily timbered mountain with implacable stone walls. We could not clear it.

The pilot turned the stick hard to the left—there was nothing else he could do—forcing the plane into a turn beyond its design capabilities. The plane lost its lift and stalled over the river. I could hear the smooth roar of its motor, trying vainly to pull us upward. Then the black frames of an impossible film began rolling in slow motion and the blinding speed of light at the same time. The last domino had fallen.

Now I understood: It was not OK. We would crash in Trotter's Pool.

Just before the end, with the Cessna over on its side and falling rapidly, a final word was spoken, a simple profanity, the most human sound I have ever heard. It was the pilot, cursing softly.

I glanced quickly at my old friend sitting in the front seat; he was quiet and firm and said nothing. From the corner of my eye I saw my back-seat companion brace himself as we fell from the sky as if we had no wings at all.

The river came up as if in a dream, all silver, green and translucent gold. Boulders appeared in the current like giant nuggets. Even then, in that final transcendent moment, the river seemed beautiful and familiar, an old friend.

How could it kill us? Maybe it would be OK. We'd land in the river and swim for it. It wouldn't be that bad. The water would cushion our fall.

Then the river exploded inside the plane with a shower of splintered glass and a series of fantastic distorted images.

From the abyss that followed, a dark room came slowly into focus. I tried to make sense of what I saw; it appeared to be a shadowy group of card players gathering around submerged stones in the river. I sat down to join them. On the far side of the stone table was a form I couldn't quite make out. It looked like a piece of ledgerock with moss growing out of it, stringy and waving in the current. In a way, it looked like hair. Someone's hair.

Jesus. Where was I?

No one answered, and I looked up at the sky through ten feet of cold water. White clouds passed silently overhead, floating beyond a tangled web of steel and glass. My stomach felt funny. Something was crawling into my body, feeling me, testing and probing as it went deeper and deeper. It must be a spider, one that was feeding from the feel of it.

Suddenly I remembered folding myself into the back of the pilot's seat, trying to protect my face, then swallowing blood and losing it in the river. And then I found the pilot, completely submerged and already gone. I remember how soft his hair was, and how young he felt as I ran my hands over his lifeless body still strapped in its seat, slumped over the stick like a cold scarecrow.

A great sadness came. He was just a kid doing his job. He should have had a priest or someone to comfort him when he died. Fifty miles away his wife was probably cooking for their four-year-old daughter, neither yet aware her husband or father had just perished.

I held his head in prayer, then looked for my two friends, spitting out teeth while I groped my way through a kerosene slick full of things too horrible to consider. Then the feeding spider reached my legs and consumed what little strength remained. As I left the crumpled aluminum fuselage, I realized I was wounded beyond my darkest imaginings. I was dying.

How could this be happening? I was simply a fisherman on a holiday.

Moments later I found myself lying on the shore next to a pool of muddy water where I had once fished, a place where I'd always worried about roll casts and drifting flies. Now I was splitting into a million fragments and fading away from myself.

So many things passed through my mind: glimpses of family and friends and all the trappings, accumulations, ambitions and desires of a lifetime, all now dropping away, shot to hell, until only a single thought remained: that of my wife, my life's partner. I remember thinking my last conscious thought would be of her.

There was no way of knowing that a quarter mile downriver, around a dogleg of rapids, guests at the lodge had heard the sound of the Cessna going down. Jerrie Lou Wickwire rushed to start the jet boat. She was crying; she already knew how bad it could be. It was the guides' day off and they were all out fishing; whatever happened next was up to her.

Someone ripped a door from one of the cabins to serve as a stretcher. The news went out to Smithers on channel eight. Tom Brooks, chief pilot for Canadian Helicopters, took the call from Jerrie Lou.

"Tom," she said, "the Central Mountain charter is down in the river."

Strange. The radio-telephone hadn't worked for five days, defying every effort to fix it; yet it worked instantly when the emergency call went out.

I had maybe twenty minutes left when Jerrie Lou and the others found me on the rocks, drifting in and out of consciousness. Shadows moved through my mind; the spider, now in my ear, whispered to me. "Don't worry," it said. "I'm almost finished. You won't feel a thing."

I wondered what it would do with me. Had I lived a good life? Was this the hour of judgment? What would the verdict be?

No answer. Even the natural world, which I had always loved and which had been my sanctuary since I was a small boy, held no answer this time: nothing in the wind or the river, nor any sign from the surrounding stones and trees.

I was lying on my stomach, down like a torn flag in the cold mud and the stones, an ex-hippy turned middle-aged fisherman bleeding to death in British Columbia, still trying to figure it all out. My face was horribly deformed and my heart didn't know what to do next. I had lost my front teeth, ruptured an eye and broken an arm and a leg. One ear was almost ripped off and I was sliced from head to toe by all that damned glass and steel. And my two friends and the pilot were all somehow, sadly, dead.

I felt myself bleeding to death one heartbeat at a time, suspended and lost in a landscape without beginning or end, without form or dimension. A great fear came up inside me, the greatest I have ever known, a fear impossible to contain. I could also feel the eager mouth of the feeding spider, the warmth of its saliva, the brush of its hair on my face.

Then, almost imperceptibly at first, I sensed something approaching, coming from all directions at once, something so far beyond ordinary definition it defied all logic and reason. It spoke to me, the voice of another being, but one I could not name. The voice seemed to resonate within me, all the way down to my soul, and suddenly I was no longer afraid. Whoever or whatever it was became a light brighter than a star, curling around me, and I yielded to bliss. I suppose if you pressed me for a name, I would simply have to say that it was whatever we call God who came to me in that moment; I don't know who or what else to call it.

"I have come to help you," the voice told me, "because you cannot stay here. You are someplace you cannot remain, and for which there is no name I can give you. Do you understand?"

"Yes," I thought I heard myself saying. "What comes next? Am I dead?"

"No, not yet. You are between shadow and light, between life and not living, but you cannot stay here. You must choose one or the other. You must go on dying or return where you came from. The choice is yours."

Suddenly I realized the choice was mine. It was my turn to know the truth, and it would be so easy. So damn easy. "Child's play," I thought.

Why not go for it? I was no longer afraid of dying. There was nothing to fear. And I realized something else, perhaps the greatest discovery of all, perhaps the source of all faith: I knew that if I died, I would be eternally conscious, in some new and strange way, and I would be absorbed into this incredible being who was speaking to me, -earning everything as I passed. I could be this way forever.

It was tempting. I didn't need my body any more; it lay like an empty sack on the shore of Trotter's Pool.

How could I go back? How could I even find the way? Did I even want to go back?

I can't tell you now exactly why I decided to go on living, or how I managed it—only that I was somehow given the knowledge and power to control myself at a level I would never have thought possible had I not experienced it. Thus guided, I found my way through a strange wind that seemed to blow between two worlds and navigated a labyrinth of tunnels and doors that opened as I asked them to, determined to return, to re-focus and live life as best I could.

It didn't take long. My next memory was of watching from a pile of Dacron sleeping bags as the four walls of the lodge seemed to grow out of the earth and mortise into place like the sides of a wooden box. Photographs, windows and paintings appeared on the walls in a flash of light; the ceiling came down from heaven and clicked into place. I could smell the autumn air. The river returned to my ears in a rush of familiar sound, just outside the cabin door.

A ring of faces circled me and I was a like a fetus lying on the tabletop, wrapped up in a fiberglass cocoon for the flight back. Again I heard a voice, only this time it belonged to a doctor from Kansas who was a guest at the lodge and was fighting to save my life.

"We're losing him," the voice said. "Dammit, his heart is going."

"It's OK, I can fix that," I remember saying.

"Well, son," he said, "if you can, you'd better do it now."

When the emergency plane landed at Smithers a medical team was waiting, including the world's friendliest nurse. She caught me just as I porpoised momentarily into consciousness, took one look and asked, "Jeez, Honey, how in the hell did you get out of the fire?"

"What fire?" I asked. "There was no fire."

"Oh, God. You're as black as coal. They're hematomas; your whole body is . . . Oh, jeez. We can't give you any medication. We need to know everywhere it hurts, so tell me, where does it hurt?"

"I don't have any pain. It doesn't hurt."

She took my hand. "Oh yeah? Well, Sweety, everything you have is going to hurt soon, and it's going to hurt for a long time."

They went to work, with needles and thread and other instruments, and kept on working until 10:00 that night, without giving me any pain killers, as the nurse had said. She stayed with me, my only remaining contact with the world of men, doctors, and fish. She was sweetly nervous, not knowing if I was going to live or die while I tried to do whatever she asked—mostly attempting to regulate my heartbeat or breathe whenever the lines on the monitor jumped around too much. Meanwhile the doctors kept stitching and pulling out shards of glass.

Around 10:30, when they were finished, she gently squeezed my arm in the dark of my room, then left with a tear shining in her eye.

She was right. It was beginning to hurt. I pounded the morphine button.

I learned later that I had somehow escaped from the plane just before it finally went under, taking Daniel Hellston, Anton Holter and Donald Payne with it.

Now, sometimes when I am on the river all alone, they come back to me. It can happen anytime, anywhere—but most often, as it has this time, when I am fishing on Trotter's Pool, where they died.

They emerge from the shadows and trees beyond the stretch I am fishing, and I hear the click of stones as they approach the place where I stand in the shallows, waiting. Without embarrassment I hold them each in my arms and try to say all the things I never had the chance to say on the day they left me. There is much to be said.

They are healed and beautiful. Their eyes hold a light that brings a feeling of peace unlike any other. We turn to face the pool together, four friends united by a beautiful river and dreams unknown to others.

The early morning sun is on the water, shining through a mist that slowly leaves the river and lifts into the air. It rises above us, past the spruce, hemlock and cottonwood, past the soaring wings of ravens and ospreys, going ever higher, even beyond the tiny speck of a distant eagle, and merges finally with the silver clouds floating far away in the sky.

"The Shadow Knows"

Let's face it. There are three and only three segments in an angler's life: The First Part, the Middle Part, and the Last Part. Defining the boundaries separating the three segments represents some risk although serious and repeated attempts to do so are clear evidence that you have yet to escape the Middle Part, the least important of the three. The Middle is the least important for several reasons, but mostly because counting, naming and separating things and events into categories, some of which are morally defined, is now irresistible. There is, for example, "Oh good Lord, Robert, I thought you knew. Yes, it's bamboo and I'm fly fishing only!" Or... "To hell with 'em Bubba...(a pause and a steaming spit...) those 'muthafuggers' never catch anything. A bunch of creeps."

It also rains a lot in the middle, the waters muddied by competition and infatuation with the various indexes and symbols of success—including, but not limited to, fantastic collections of paraphenalia, name dropping and (my own favorite weakness) the belief that the farther you travel, the better they are and the harder they pull. And last, but not least, the middle is smothered by the unbridled belief that of course, all of this will last forever.

The Last Part? Anything can happen in the Last Part. At any time. Including redemption from the sins of The Middle. (There are no sins in The First Part). The Last Part always begins with such events as looking carefully and with great understanding at the tree before you turn and start your back cast, then snagging it three times in a row, in exactly the same place as your New Zealand guide descends the tree each time, faithfully re-ties your terminal rig, and then climbs back up to show you where to put the next one, as you stand there waiting like an expectant loon. Or, you are at a party and in the dim light you are unable to distinguish the host's sleeping cat from the patch of moose hide he uses for tying steelhead flies. And at some point during The Last Part—if you are lucky or very wise—when you look at a fish, a river, passing clouds, your annual stock report, or a woman, you finally think about something other than yourself.

And the First Part? A biased opinion: it may be the wisest; it is certainly the most democratic. Carp and Atlantic salmon if encountered, would speak the same language and each would have equal opportunity to attain the status of trophies and if large enough, either would certainly be worth a good pee in the pants. Tackle? Rubber worms are fine, as are frozen guts, bleached pork rind sauteed in formaldehyde and fishing with "poles." Anything goes. It's being there that counts. Not a bad idea. Most importantly, the First Part is the first immersion and baptism into water and biology, the attraction of the body, mind and soul to the mud, blood and current of the sport. It is the sudden discovery of truth, magic. If you are lucky this soon becomes religion. And now, suddenly, you're getting somewhere.

My own First Part began in Southern Missouri some fifty-eight years ago, and if the sins of the father are visited upon the son, so are the blessings. I caught my first fish on a trip with my father and it was love at first sight, the equal of any trophy I would later encounter. Anywhere. Any time. The event materialized in a warm, muddy summer creek at the point where a small tributary joined the mainstem. According to everyone else, meaning my cousins and all, the small channel catfish was not large enough to deserve the title of a true channel; but that mattered little to me. Nor did the choice of tackle. The four inch trophy fell prey to a nine foot bamboo pole, a short shank of braided line as thick as parachute cord and a six inch leader of approximately fifty pound test.

The polite implications of catch-and-release are also lost on young boys with their first fish, as well they should be. On the other hand, death was out of the question. I simply couldn't kill it. The whiskered, shovel-headed channel catfish was perceived as a friend and in some ways a kindred spirit, although at the time I had no idea where such a sentiment came from. So the catfish was placed in my father's aluminum minnow bucket where it circled in ever-tightening spirals, like a small brown submarine-bird without wings. Eventually, about a week later, it came to rest in the very center of the pail, upside down and quite dead, floating in a posture I found horrifying.

I found the fish's death impossible to integrate with the excitement I had experienced in catching it. So it remained in the minnow bucket for some time, still dead, unmoving despite my desperate attempts to revive it with fresh water, bread crumbs, small pieces of chicken or anything else I could pirate from the kitchen.

As it turned out, my mother, who was in charge of both the kitchen and religion in our home, provided the necessary moral escape. Her words had the ring of freedom, the path out of the dark oblivion I sensed and for which I felt responsible. She told me that if I stopped feeding the fish things it didn't want and put it in the ground, it would go instantly to catfish heaven. And in this way I was introduced to the possibilities of welding the impulses and responsibilities of angling to those of religion, a notion that remains with me to this day. I still have no use for either one without the simultaneous presence of the other.

As a six-year-old I was quick to see the possibilities; I lost no time praying for another catfish, for model airplanes, Tom Mix six-shooters with bandoleers of silver bullets and, eventually, a certain girl named Beverly. In later years the scope of my petitions expanded to include Atlantic salmon, permit, a dark-eyed beauty of Italian descent who taught school, trucks, African Ridgebacks, and as many steelhead over twenty pounds as I could possibly handle.

My father remained my fishing coach for years, although always distantly. He was a storyteller, a guitar player who had his own band, a man who hunted and fished wherever and whenever he wished, and one who sometimes seemed disinterested in the affairs of his family. He was also a hopeless womanizer. My response to these traits was immediate: I worshipped him.

He knew more about hunting than anyone I ever met and pursued it most of his life, seeking ducks and geese and later deer and elk, for which he had a genuine passion. When it came to fishing, he spoke with intensity and excitement as he explained its complexities, although I realized many years later he didn't know as much about it as he said he did. But he wasn't a liar; he was a teller of stories. His words were saturated with passion and enthusiasm and triggered images of river-bottom swamps in rural Mississippi, dark nights spent haunting the bayous, and the whistle of birds migrating along the central flyways of the landscapes he called home when he was a boy. He spoke of warm leaves crackling underfoot on autumn hunts and the reflected light of sunsets on the waters he knew and I wanted to know. In truth I wanted to be more than his son; I also wanted to be his fishing and hunting buddy, and I dreamed of going with him. For better or worse, I devoted much of my youth trying to convince him to take me along to the places of which he spoke.

I had some success, but always wished for more. Almost to the day of his death he remained distant, removed and unconnected, but in the end we finally made it as buddies. I suppose that's the best of it, and perhaps it matters less when a father and son find one another, than whether they do.

My mother was German, stubborn and strong in most ways. She worked hard and without complaint. She loved to sew and make things—home decorations, fishing shirts, even flannel sacks for fly rods or shotguns, spun magically from an old treadle sewing machine. Her fingers were beautiful and her eyes full of light and unlimited patience.

From the beginning she knew how much I loved fishing and everything surrounding the sport and she put up with my obsession, even when I returned well after dark and found her worried that some harm had come to me. Sometimes she would cry and fuss in a way that made me nervous despite my arguments that her fears were groundless. "What could ever happen to me?" I used to ask.

My brother and sister were different. They were twins, two forks of the same river, and they shared a bond obvious to anyone who looked. Neither took to the outdoor life as a child, although I tried hard to convince my brother that fishing was the only certain way to a life of satisfaction and redemption from inevitable human frailties and the weakness of flesh—this despite his efforts to convince me the same was true of organized, waterless religion. He never fished or hunted, but I still loved him, even though I finally gave up hope of ever having him for a fishing partner.

My sister was the most clever of us and in some ways the most tenacious. She probably would have made the best angler if she had tried. She did get into fishing later in life, with a friend who drank too much, and they would tear the hell out of a few high mountain lakes in Northern California with an inexhaustible supply of sugar-cured salmon eggs and a spinning rod capable of separating a tarpon from its scales. I went to see her one time and asked if she had been doing any fishing.

"Oh yes, I have, Big Boy," she said. "Big Boy" was something she rarely called me and when she did, I paid attention. I followed her to the garage where she kept a freezer. When I looked inside I saw so many pairs of frozen trout eyes staring vacantly back at me I couldn't count them all. She read my mind. "133," she said, matter-of-factly. "I'm not into catch and release, you know."

"I hadn't noticed," I replied.

These memories of my family seem far away now, a distant patch of clouds and sunshine, partly shaped by my own distance and brooding, my obsession for fishing and my hopeless desire to weld us all together. In the end we all remained strangers, but we had our moments.

Some of the best of those moments were spent around the radio, an old brown model situated precisely in the center of one of my mother's hand-made linen place mats, or "doilies" as she called them. My favorite program was a weekly drama of danger, intrigue, murder, kidnapping and suspense, followed inevitably by salvation at the hands of the one and only Lamont Cranston, otherwise known as "The Shadow." I was spellbound by Cranston's ability to make himself completely invisible. It didn't seem to matter that he neither fished nor hunted; he was an honest man who took care of business and he soon became my public hero.

With little more than the world's most intimidating voice and his own two hands, The Shadow seemed capable of completely rearranging the moral order of a world threatened by crime and human despair, saving helpless victims from demonic villains the police could never apprehend. I can still hear his raspy voice asking The Question: "Who knows what evil lurks in the hearts of men? The Shadow knows, heh, heh, heh."

For a while I tried to make my father jealous by proclaiming The Shadow was my hero and I wanted to be just like him when I grew up, but my father didn't buy it. He knew better. And he remained where he was—just beyond the grip of a six-year-old heart coupled to an imagination that was suddenly awakening.

One night, halfway through one of the radio episodes—just at the moment Lamont escaped his corporeal container and disappeared into the world of crime and despair—my brother disappeared upstairs. Minutes later The Shadow's battle against the forces of evil was interrupted by the scent of blistering varnish and clouds of black smoke. My brother had set the house on fire.

As we stood outside watching, the fire department arrived in a swarm of lacquered red trucks and brilliant flashing lights. The water from the firehoses almost flattened the house as we watched—some of us in pajamas—in front of all the neighbors. In some ways, although I never admitted it, I thought it was an invigorating sight, something I could not have imagined, and the best example of innocent pyrotechnics I would ever witness.

Meanwhile my brother was nowhere to be found. My mother feared the worst. My father did too, although he said nothing about it and appeared merely angry, which was indeed something to be feared. The thought crossed my mind that my brother had learned "whatever evil lurks in the hearts of men" and like a shadow had simply disappeared. But he finally surfaced in the dirty laundry inside a closet. He looked like a small owl about to fly away.

Not much later my sister was struck by a drunk driver and her leg was badly broken. My mother's relatives arrived the next week and moved in to help soothe her spirit. Their laundry hung like clouds in all the spare rooms and hallways of a home about to explode.

All this proved too much for my father. He came home one evening and announced he had accepted a promotion from his company which meant moving to the West Coast.

"We're going to California," he said. "You'll all love it. It's warm all the time and beautiful. It never rains and the money grows on trees." I watched the color drain from my mother's face.

"Besides," my father continued, raising his voice and moving forward to the very edge of his chair, "they have mule deer there the size of Colorado elk, and trout as long as your arm. So help me God." With that final oath, the one he always used when he was fibbing, he forked his vegetables down his gullet with one hand and doubled the other into a clinched fist that struck an emphatic blow for freedom on the surface of the dining room table.

My mother muttered something under her breath and I could visualize my father hanging from a limb like a gutted deer, skinned and lifeless, tongue drooping in the breeze.

That night the sun set on a family in temporary disrepair. I listened to the argument through walls that seemed as if they were made of paper. My sister was also awake and each time my mother made a point she would signal support by banging her plaster cast on the floor—a thundering mantra of banging plaster coupled with the wail of her thin voice, one which lasted the entire night.

Just before dawn, everything finally settled down and I could hear my parents making up and making plans. California? What in the hell was that? What in the hell was a mule deer? Who would want to shoot anything that looked like a donkey? Even the arm-length trout were losing their appeal.

I thought about Beverly. Beverly the beautiful, only two seats away in the second grade. Beverly with hair the color of the rising sun and the sweetest of all smiles. How could I ever live without her? We were supposed to go see the puppet show next month. Now what?

With that last thought, the universe unfolded, then doubled back on itself. Constellations of light and swirling dust poured through my room, and the first light of approaching day threw long shadows and angular patterns that danced along the floor, then moved quickly up the walls with a soft, tangerine light. But the room was still half dark and in the dim light one shadow appeared eerily different and out of place. I watched as it moved around the room, circling silently, gliding effortlessly like a hawk in a high wind, finally coming to rest on the ceiling like a black umbrella from another world.

"Who, or maybe I should say, what are you?" I asked in a small, quivering voice.

"I think you already know who I am," came the reply from the dark umbrella.

"Uh . . . well, I'm not so sure. What do you want of me?" I was trying to be brave and held onto my legs, which wanted desperately to carry me as far away as possible.

"I came because you needed me and because I know you are afraid," the voice said. "I am The Shadow."

Click. Just like that. No radio, nothing but the sound of that voice, the wind through the curtains, and the early cry of locusts in the maple trees on the street below.

The Shadow. The Shadow himself. I felt a euphoric rush of relief, a flash of electricity not unlike that which had come through the line when I hooked the catfish. Suddenly it became obvious. I was certain that I was going to be the first kid on my block—and in fact the whole world—to circumvent the globe hand-in-hand with my hero, The Shadow.

I knew what the itinerary would be. The first stop would be for a moral adjustment long overdue. I would materialize through the wall of Eddie Rodriguez's house. Eddie had laughed when he learned my catfish had died in the tin bucket. To hell with him; I'd look him in the eye and urinate on him, and while he was still trying to decide exactly what had happened, I'd spin around and hit the candy store for a whole bag of Snickers. From there, who knew? Africa perhaps, or maybe back to the river for another catfish.

"Can I call you Lamont?" I asked enthusiastically.

"No, you can't," the voice replied. "That's impossible. Just pay attention and listen carefully. I know you have a lot of questions, but first I need to know something about you. How old are you?"

"Six and three quarters."

"That's good. That's perfect," he said. "Well then, I'll try to explain some things."

"Wait a minute," I said. "Who sent you?"

For a moment there was no response, only the most profound silence I had ever known, but then the answer finally came: "Oh, let's just say that a certain part of you sent me."

I didn't understand that and I wondered if the guy was crazy. Of course I didn't say so out loud, because you never know what a shadow will do if you say the wrong thing, or even look at it the wrong way; it might become invisible.

Then I realized what The Shadow had meant. It had to do with imagination. "Oh, that part of me," I said.

The Shadow read my mind as if it were his own and told me to mark the moment well, for it was the beginning of something new and once it began I could never go back again. I thought of the yellow bamboo pole still hanging from the rafters of the garage, and the catfish swimming around and around in the bucket. I thought of a whole life of fishing.

"I understand," I told him. "I'm in."

"Good, but we need to hurry now, because there isn't much time left. So ask me anything you need to know before it's too late."

And that was how it started. For the next hour I asked every important question I could think of—about the locusts that came each summer from nowhere I could see, the faces I saw in clouds, the clouds I saw in faces, where music comes from, where worms go when it rains, what frogs believe, how to talk to Beverly, and what were rainbow trout? Did they come out of the sky with those colors or were they born with them?

At first The Shadow only smiled at the questions, but then he began to answer them, and as he spoke the morning grew brighter and moved through the room in a great swirl of galactic dust. Water rushed through the room, the water of lakes and rivers and blue oceans still unfished, and The Shadow came down from his perch on the ceiling and moved steadily closer to me until he was at the side of my bed with the very tip of his voice wrapped around a fold in the wrinkled sheet. I knew then he would be going soon, out the window or to some other place I could not follow. To the place of locusts, perhaps. Or catfish in buckets.

"Always take care of your family and those you love even if you don't understand them," he said, "because these things matter most, more than anything else, and the rest of it can go to hell, and probably will, wherever that is."

"I know where it is," I said. "It's in Eddie Rodriguez. I hate him."

"Well, you might be right, but there isn't much you can do about it. Those things have to change by themselves and it takes a long time, longer than you have, that's for sure. So just be patient and help when you can. One day it will happen."

"Yes, but who are people, really?" I asked. "I mean, if you had to say just one thing about them that was true all the time and which answered everything, what would you say?" This was something I had always wanted to know, as I found people, even my own family, to be unpredictable and mysterious. Worse, they often seemed crazy.

The Shadow said nothing for a moment, and as the warmth of the rising sun passed through me, I watched him move a little farther, going more to my right side until he came to rest softly in my right hand, no longer a shadow at all but a point of light, a small point, as small as a drop of water.

"They are your reflection," he whispered softly.

I was quiet for a moment, thinking about what I had just heard, although at that moment, I wasn't sure what it meant. But I had one more question.

"What about getting old and dying?" I asked. "Will that happen to me? What will it be like?"

There was no answer, but the curtains moved even as I was uttering the words, and something suddenly passed by, reflected briefly in the mirror by the nightstand. It looked like a sparrow, but I couldn't be sure, and when I looked to The Shadow for interpretation or help, it was too late; he had disappeared in a flash of light, vanishing into the growing brightness of the new day, just as you would expect of a shadow.

The next night I sat by myself under the haunting light of black iron lanterns in front of my house, like I always did in the summer, watching the world go by from a curbside row of walnut trees. The locusts were singing in the heat of the evening, and fireflies flashed with sparkling points of green and yellow light. Overhead the stars were starting to come out, and as I looked down at the curb, I saw a young bird, a baby sparrow that had fallen from its nest. It lay in the gutter with a crooked little mouth, torn feathers and eyes that were closed. It was upside down, just as I was, all alone, wings outstretched as if for balance, lying next to some leaves in a cold puddle of water left by the street cleaners. I thought of the bird's descent to earth, the sadness of it, its first and only flight, with wings that didn't yet work, eyes not yet open as it fell from the sky like a stone. And I felt something move inside myself.

I couldn't leave the bird there like that; it wasn't right. So I carried it into the backyard to the place where I had buried the catfish. Maybe they could be friends, I thought. Even if they were dead. Maybe it wouldn't matter. I just didn't want the bird to be alone. Nobody should be alone, I thought.

After I finished burying the sparrow I looked and listened for a long time, but the only sounds were of the garden gate squeaking in the wind. I stood up, carefully, and as I passed through the gate everything changed. I felt something new in myself. Suddenly I was connected to the whole world. My heart soared. My loneliness disappeared. I had found the essential chord, and no further questions seemed necessary. Only the joy of living remained; I found no sorrow in this—only opportunity.

The Shadow was right. Everything was a reflection. Mine and theirs; us and them, it and not-it. From that day on, I vowed, my kinfolk would include not only a family I did not always understand, but such things as walnut trees, fireflies, catfish, and who knows what else? Even dead birds and Eddie Rodriguez. Boundaries dissolved, genders blurred, specific political persuasions, religions and philosophies meant nothing, and yet whatever might happen along the way and before the end, was somehow understandable, necessary and unavoidable, for whatever reason. All of it. Oh boy. The entire enchilada.

Today I see these things most clearly when I fish and take the time to think about them, and that has made all the difference. Is life only a River of Dreams? Who knows?

Perhaps The Shadow knows.

Not long after that my father kept his word and moved us away from the farm ponds and warm-water creeks of southern Missouri.

Although I never caught another catfish like that first one, it still worked out for the best because I found a new world of high Western mountains and evergreen forests, places where I could see the turn of a speckled trout feeding silently, floating above the earth in a sky of clear water, alive and beautiful, and these places became my addiction of blood and soul, my life's salvation. In all three Parts.

Steelhead Fever

The Klamath River comes to life north of the Oregon border and well east of the Siskiyou Mountains. It's shallow at first, a summer stream more than anything else, with scattered sagebrush and warm desert sand along its banks. Then it leaves the desert and enters thick stands of cottonwood and pine, reflecting their tall silhouettes in pleasing contrast to the slate-gray gravel bars and sienna-colored hills.

Somewhere near a place called Horse Creek, then east and south past Somes Bar and Orleans, down to the Hoopa Indian reservation in California, the river slowly begins to gather strength and its real nature is revealed in deep canyons and gorges, broad tailouts and dancing riffles. Boiling currents rise to the surface, then disappear only to re-emerge downstream, and the river seems to tear itself apart on stubborn boulders and slick granite ledges. If you can wade here, you can wade anywhere—with due apologies to the North Umpqua.

After welcoming a multitude of small feeder creeks and tributaries, including the once-majestic Trinity, the mighty Klamath finally reaches the Pacific with a push of water so powerful it seems nothing could stop it. If the late fall rains continue into winter, then nothing can; the river lifts up in great floods that easily topple 2,000-year-old redwoods. But if the rains end when they are supposed to end, the river rises only enough to summon back the schools of salmon and steelhead that call the Klamath home.

Once these runs were spectacular. Today, sadly, they are only mediocre—if you measure by numbers. But the fish that remain are still magnificent.

The Klamath is a river of legends, birthplace of stories about fish and fishermen, hidden gold and grim murder, and—sometimes—enchanting women. Over the years some of these tales reached the ears of prominent angling authors such as Zane Grey, Clark Van Fleet, Ted Trueblood and others, and their writings helped popularize the river. By the late 1940s the word was out: the Klamath had a run of wild steelhead that was something special, a silver horde that annually filled both the river and its narrow feeder creeks, an army of traveling fish as great as any in the world.

Famous fly patterns evolved along the fabled runs of Happy Camp, Seiad Valley, Orleans and such—the Burlap, Silver Hilton, Orleans Barber, Brindle Bug and others. Champion distance casters from San Francisco's venerable Golden Gate Angling and Casting Club covered the river with homemade lines carefully spliced according to secret formulas. Their casts rocketed over pools stuffed with steelhead up to ten pounds, including the world-famous smaller Klamath fish known as "half-pounders."

By the mid-1950s the Klamath had become an important piece of the West Coast steelhead pie. The fever had become an epidemic; legions of anglers gathered each autumn for fishing so easy it required several ice chests to satisfy their appetites. It seemed the whole world loved the Klamath and wanted to fish it.

That a river of such abundance could infect ordinary men with steelhead fever is understandable; that it could inspire the writing and attention of several generations of American anglers is understandable, too. That its influence could eventually reach into places as unlikely as the smoky steelyards and shipbuilding plants of Richmond, California, is a little more difficult to understand—but it did.

There, in the mid-1950s, amid iron girders, noon whistles, and sheets of cold rolled steel, labored a steelhead angler named Leroy Higgins. Leroy was a welder and weekend miner who could barely read or write, but he had an incredibly keen sense of hearing. His best friend and fishing companion, an elderly steelhead fiend known only as Gramps, loved the pleasures of the grape as much as those of rod and reel. And it's with these two unlikely characters that this story really begins.

The year was 1953. *Sports Afield, Field & Stream* and *Outdoor Life* were all reporting the "new" West Coast angling phenomenon called "Steelhead—the King of Trouts." Some of these reports, in which the Klamath River was mentioned prominently, somehow penetrated Leroy Higgins' consciousness. From there, during the course of lunchtime conversations, they were transmitted to the willing ears of my father. Anything was fair game in those discussions, including how to get rich without working any harder than necessary, where to find the best deer hunting (a tie between Plumas and Alturas Counties) or the best frogging (Calaveras County, where you could still shoot frogs at night from a boat, using a flashlight tied to the barrel of a .22 long rifle). And, of course, steelhead fishing.

At that time the State of California also offered interesting opportunities for do-it-yourself miners. Free mining claims were available on state-owned lands in the Trinity, Salmon and Klamath watersheds. All you had to do was provide evidence of the existence of gold on the land—"showing color," it was called. Once a tract had shown color, you could stake a claim and explore further. But there was a catch: To show the claim was being actively worked, you had to make minimal improvements to the claim in each of the next five years. These were to be reported in a filing called a "Proof of Labor." After five years of such "improvements" the claim was yours for the next ninety years, but if you failed to make the required improvements the claim would revert to the state.

Leroy and Gramps already had such a claim, overlooking the Klamath River near the town of Orleans. As they described it to my father, the claim was accessible via a narrow logging road not far from the Ishi-Pishi bridge. The bridge spanned a particularly nasty section of turbulent water and granite ledge-rock "where the Injuns dump the bodies of white men they don't like," according to Leroy. These victims reportedly included a local game warden who was forced off the road into the black waters one night by parties unknown. His "crime" had been an effort to enforce fish and game regulations on a local population that cared very little about such things and didn't believe in their necessity. They never found the warden's body, much less his truck or a willing human replacement for the officer.

Gramps and Leroy fit comfortably into the local population. Not only did they have a mining claim on "the best riffle on the entire river," but they maintained amicable relations with neighboring Indians, miners, loggers, Orleans tavern keepers and other characters who willingly shared inside information. For four years they also had "worked hard" making improvements to their mining claim, including construction of a fishing lodge referred to as "The Cabin." On paper this building was listed as a tool shed and office for their mining company, and it had running water, electricity, a terraced vegetable garden and a lookout post from which Leroy and Gramps someday hoped to glimpse a feeding Sasquatch or Bigfoot.

This combination paradise and fortress was described to my father as "a garden of Eden on the banks of the best steelhead river in the world, a place, goddammit, where a man can still be a man." Whenever Leroy talked like this, he would square his shoulders and cinch his belt, then spit on the ground and look as tall as he could, while Gramps nodded his head in the affirmative.

Not only that, but Leroy and Gramps had "in a bank vault somewhere—we can't say exactly where"—the clincher: the last remaining copy of an old Spanish map they had stumbled across in a feed store in Eureka. The map established the certain existence and possible location of a vein of pure gold some sixteen inches thick and 150 yards long. According to the map, and supposedly verified by Spanish and Indian legend, the vein lay buried somewhere in the vicinity of Gramps' and Leroy's claim. They felt certain it was only a matter of time before they found it.

When he heard that, my father couldn't resist an invitation to accompany them on a trip to the claim. Nor could I—even though I was only twelve years old at the time.

Gramps and Leroy came to our home one morning after the graveyard shift. This wasn't unusual; they often stopped for coffee after working the graveyard, and sat around the table sharing the latest news about the steelhead run. Usually the conversation went something like this: "The fish are stacked in there like cordwood, pass the cream and sugar please." But on this particular morning Leroy had brought the paperwork necessary for my father to file a new mining claim. Gramps produced a few nuggets he said had come from their claim and told my father he could buy them and use them to "show color" until he found some of his own. "No use wasting any time," he said. "The half-pounders will be there in a few weeks, and they'll be stacked in there like cordwood."

Plans were laid and the rush was on. The expedition would include a trailer made from sheets of steel borrowed from the scrap pile down at the plant, supported by two immense patched-up old truck tires. Hitched behind Leroy's 1950 Plymouth station wagon, the trailer would carry all necessary supplies. According to my father, this trip would be the opportunity of a lifetime: first to strike it rich, then to learn first-hand how to catch big steelhead from two undisputed masters of the Klamath. My mother seemed less impressed by the possibilities, but those were the days when a woman's place was in the kitchen and children were to be seen and not heard. So neither she nor I said anything, although I was certain I'd soon have enough money to buy a new fishing rod and at least a dozen shiny lures.

We started out near the end of August. I remember looking into the trailer before we left just to see what supplies were needed to strike it rich and catch fish. There wasn't much: four shovels, three rusty spinning rods, five boxes of Aunt Jemima pancake mix, a large black iron skillet, four sleeping bags, some lard, a box of condoms and two cases of Gallo sauterne, nine gallons to the case.

I did some quick figuring. The trip was supposed to last four or five days. When would we fish? How many pancakes can one man eat? And what about the condoms? Perhaps, I thought, they were to be filled with sand and used as sinkers, much as Sacramento River Delta anglers used empty Bull Durham tobacco pouches.

Gramps reintroduced himself to me in the driveway, next to the trailer, extending one hand while he clutched a gallon jug in the other. "I believe in being polite to my friends," he said. "I toast them everywhere I go, especially on fishing and mining trips. So here's to you, young man." He gargled a swig while I shook his hand, and then we both climbed into the back seat of the Plymouth. Gramps would be my stagecoach partner for the long journey north, seated on the other side of a spring that was emerging like a coiled reptile through the plastic seat cover.

The plan was simple. Gramps would drink. My father and Leroy would drive. I didn't know what was expected of me, and I knew better than to ask, but it didn't really matter; I was in the car and on the team headed for the summit. I began to count my new lures. Maybe I'd buy three dozen.

It was an eleven or twelve-hour drive from the Bay Area to the Klamath in those days. Gramps toasted everything along the way: road signs, trees, birds, left turns (he was left-handed), certain cloud formations, mountains with snow, mountains without, and license plates from states he liked. "Friends are where you find them," he remarked as these things passed by. Road signs were his favorite because they were the most frequent and reliable subjects for toasting. He would spy a sign that said "Passing OK" or "Curves Ahead" and declare: "That's a friendly sign. I'll drink to that."

It was one hell of a ride. Gramps took a break from toasting long enough to teach me how to tie a good clinch knot, substituting the handle of his glass jug for the eye of a hook and using some rope for the leader. He was toasted himself by the time we reached Red Bluff, but you would never have known it. "That's because my blood is fifty-proof," he said, as I practiced the knot and he resumed saluting his many friends.

Red Bluff went by in a swirl of dust and an energetic toast, and we started a long, winding lift through rolling hills, scrub oak, scattered pine and red manzanita. By evening the landscape had changed to mountains and looming towers of evergreen, sentinels pointing the way to waters wild and free, the home of chinook salmon, native rainbow trout and, rarest of all, steelhead. It wouldn't be long before I'd see one, I thought.

We reached the Klamath and The Cabin around midnight. The river lay far below in the lightless dark, how far I didn't know. Leroy, Gramps and my father moved in and out of the headlights of the Plymouth like ghosts, carrying supplies from the trailer to The Cabin. I was ready to start fishing, but my father said it was too dark, so I put down my rod and went to investigate The Cabin—House of Eden, sanctuary of sanctuaries, "The Place, Goddammit!" In the dim light I made out an old trailer pressed against the hillside like a deflated blimp. The roof slumped in the middle like an aluminum camel with two humps. Ragged curtains hung like dirty gauze in windows without glass. Where was the fly-tying room, the rod rack, the books on steelhead fishing?

"Ain't she a beauty?" Gramps asked as he toasted the trailer, then fell backward through the parallel beams of light emanating from the Plymouth. No, that's not quite right; he didn't fall, he simply descended gently to earth like a bird landing, already asleep and smiling. I looked again at the cabin; it seemed smaller the longer I looked, and in my mind it no longer warranted capital letters. It was surrounded by crumpled tin cans and rusty piles of miscellaneous junk, including the oxidized skeleton of a plow, an old washtub, and other items beyond recognition. I held my breath as Leroy invited me inside.

It smelled like a dead whale. The floor was barely attached to the walls and sloped about twenty degrees so that it was hard to remain standing. Litter had been swept under iron bunk beds at each end of the cold, damp room. The bunks had springs but no mattresses. An old wooden table stood in the center of the room, leaning hard toward the north. The room served as kitchen, dining hall, living quarters and bedroom. An outhouse had been sandwiched onto one end of the trailer almost as an afterthought.

"Rats and mice, goddammit!" Leroy cursed, flashing his trusty Ray-O-Vac. "I can hear 'em. Never mind, we'll get 'em in the morning after breakfast." He unpacked the last three items—a Coleman gas lantern, a Smith & Wesson .38-caliber revolver and a steel case holding 500 rounds of hollow-point bullets.

"Big Foot," he said. "You never know. I think I heard one on the way in, but I didn't want to scare you." The thought crossed my mind that I would rather sleep next to a Sasquatch (of either sex) than stay in this cabin.

Next morning wasn't too bad. Leroy shot only two rounds, missing both times, but the mice got the message and stayed away for the rest of the trip. Breakfast was early and after pancakes and wild blueberries we headed out to stake my father's claim and help Gramps and Leroy with their next round of "improvements." My father had one of those honorary Southern titles of "Colonel," so we decided to name our claim "The Little Colonel." I would be listed as a junior partner.

We climbed hard up steep slopes and perspired our way through thick brush and clusters of verdant pine until we finally reached the top of a hill where we found a hole in the ground. Gramps wiped his brow and hoisted his jug to toast a squirrel on the limb just over his head.

"We gotta fill this sucker up," Leroy said, pointing at the hole.

"What do you mean?" my father asked.

"Well, goddammit, Jack," Leroy answered. "This here hole was last year's improvement. Now, we're going to fill it up. We alternate every year. One year we fill; one year we empty. They never check. You know how the government is."

Shovels appeared, one for each of us, although I was given five minutes to chase frogs out of the hole before we started. Then, for the next three hours, we shoveled. All the while I could hear the river far below and my heart ached for just one cast.

It was nearly four o'clock when we finished filling the hole, tamping the dirt down firmly—clear evidence that some real work had been done.

"Isn't it time to go fishing?" I asked.

"Hell, yes," Leroy said. "Good idea. Let's go back to the cabin and rig up."

"I'll drink to that," Gramps replied, raising his jug.

By the time we finally found the right trail and made our way back to the cabin it was dusk. I ran all the way down to the edge of the Klamath by myself, as everyone else was too tired to go fishing.

Not much happened. I can remember how strong the river looked, and how large, with boiling currents I couldn't read or understand. I cast blindly over and over again, believing in each cast like you must when (a) you don't know what you're doing or (b) even when you do, but I caught nothing.

The sun set behind the ridge and I heard Leroy's .38 go off—my signal to stop fishing and climb back up the mountain. Thus ended my first day of steelhead fishing on the Klamath. Or anywhere, for that matter.

Dinner passed uneventfully. The dishes were washed in genuine Klamath River water I hauled up the hillside in a leaky, galvanized tin pail. In those days you didn't need a permit for a campfire, so we just dug a hole in the ground, threw in some wood and poured gasoline on top of it. After the explosion, my father sat and talked with Leroy and Gramps while I took advantage of the opportunity to listen and learn about the world. The world of men, the world of steelhead.

Leroy spoke first and told us why he loved the Klamath so much. His story had everything and nothing to do with fishing. It was about a woman. No one seemed to know where she came from, where she lived or very much about her, except that she was young and beautiful, graceful and charming, and had incredible power over men. Some said her power approached the supernatural and perhaps it did, but the woman herself was real enough. Leroy and Gramps had seen her many times in the bar at the Orleans Hotel, where she appeared on Saturday nights in the antique glass mirror that had come from Europe 120 years before.

Leroy claimed the mirror was part of the cargo of a Spanish ship that sailed around Tierra del Fuego and up the California Coast during the gold rush. Those aboard the ship had come looking for the secret vein of gold which lay near his claim, he said.

Now, each steelhead season, the mysterious woman appeared in the ancient mirror every Saturday night. She was long of limb, with legs the color of milk, and her raven hair hung down to a supple waist. Her mouth was red and soft, her teeth white as pearls, and her eyes knew everything, including the secrets of a man's most forbidden desires. She could also hold her liquor.

Just at dark she would materialize as if by magic, waving to the loggers, miners, truck drivers, fishermen, trappers, cowboys, gas-station attendants, cat skinners and hide tanners who patronized the bar, each waiting and praying for just a glance from this woman who knew it all. Her name, Leroy said, was Darlene. He didn't know her last name, but I could have told him, even at the tender age of twelve, that goddesses of this sort frequently do not have one.

Everyone knew Darlene wore no underwear, Leroy said, and that was why she came to town on Saturday nights—to prove the fact to one man, and only one—The One. She would accept his offer of a drink and after a modest amount of conversation they would leave together for her secret mountain lair. There, in the sanctuary of her cabin, the fortunate male would experience ecstasies beyond imagination. Darlene was reputed to know at least 500 ways to a man's heart. Her wild acrobatic maneuvers always began with a nude moonlight swim in the Klamath, after which she and her chosen partner would adjourn to the bearskin rug in front of the fire in her cabin. There they would relax together without drying off because, as everyone knew, she loved to drink water from the naked body of a man.

Leroy was determined to be that man, at least once, even if it took the rest of his life. He had been trying for seven years, he said, waiting for Darlene on Saturday nights when the leaves were orange and salmon and steelhead crowded into the river.

"I'm going to succeed this trip, you can bet on it," he promised as he passed the jug back to Gramps. The fire blazed on. The trees seemed to grin in the orange firelight and I thought I could see their limbs shaking with glee. Gramps smiled and nodded approval and my father raised his eyebrows. Then Gramps passed the jug to me. I looked at my father; he nodded and held up a single finger.

The mouth of the jug was as cold as ice and the wine as warm as my blood. As I drank, I realized this steelhead fishing business was a lot more complicated and interesting than I'd thought. I decided I liked it.

After my first and only drink of wine, I was allowed to replenish the wood in the fire. We sat there almost until dawn, listening to stories about Darlene, Big Foot, the cruel fate of an innocent game warden and much more. Sparks rose from the fire and spiraled past the pointed tips of trees into a black ceiling of sky sprinkled with stars. The forest danced in the firelight, the trees seeming to bow in perfect rhythm as Hoopa drums kept pace, pounding louder and louder in my ears, while the Klamath, deep in the canyon below us, marched on to the sea. And at some point, I came to believe the stories. All of them.

Somewhere, perhaps just beyond the edge of our warm fire, where light and dark met one another in the crack between two worlds, I sensed a silent figure watching us with large, curious eyes, a figure with hands and feet like those humans once had perhaps a million years ago. Maybe Darlene was out there, too; for all I knew, she might keep company with Sasquatches as well as men. I kept looking for them, but never saw anything.

Gramps meanwhile toasted trees and sleeping chipmunks, swallowing incomprehensible quantities of sauterne. From time to time he would stick his finger in the jug, leave his place by the fire, stagger to the edge of darkness or beyond, unzip, take care of business, mumble to himself, zip up, and come back for more.

Next morning, after breakfast, I went steelhead fishing again. Again I caught nothing. The Colorado spinner swiveled like an airplane propeller through an empty seam of water for more than an hour, which was all the time I had to fish before we headed into town. The plan was to look around, pick up some mining supplies, maybe buy another spinner, eat a hamburger, then spend the afternoon and "part of the evening" at the Orleans hotel, where Leroy planned to make his move. It was Saturday.

As it turned out, there was to be no new mining equipment and no new spinners—Leroy and Gramps still owed the hardware store sixty-seven dollars from the year before—but we did get hamburgers, and finally Leroy parked the Plymouth station wagon next to the hitching post in front of the Orleans Hotel. Being well under age, I was told to wait in the car while Leroy, Gramps and my father went into the bar.

They had to get there early to get a good seat, Leroy said. He wanted the seat just left of the antique mirror, partly because he was right-handed and partly because he said he had "a better profile from the right-hand side." I decided to keep a careful lookout because I wanted at least to see Darlene. Not that I had any illusions about my chances at the age of twelve, but I did consider the possibility that she might cross the street, peer into the station wagon and decide I was The One.

Then what? I was out of chocolate and had no credit cards, or wine. No sinkers, either.

I kept watch for hours as a progression of the thirsty and lonely, the dusty and the tired, the wealthy and the poor—whites, Indians and various combinations in all sizes, shapes and ages—passed by the station wagon on their way to the bar. I never saw Darlene, and I must have cleaned my reel fifty times. By the time darkness fell I could take it apart and put it back together again with my eyes closed. To this day I am still the only person I know who can tell you exactly how many teeth there are on the main gear of a 1953 Bache-Brown Model 14 spinning reel, right-hand wind. Sixty-five, in case you're wondering.

My father, Leroy and Gramps finally emerged from the bar about 1:00 a.m., still alive with all their teeth and no blood showing. This in itself was fortunate because the Orleans Hotel was then famous for drunken brawls that usually started when the clock next to Darlene's mirror registered midnight. But on this particular Saturday night Darlene hadn't shown up.

Gramps and Leroy were well glued but my father was not. He never drank much and he was as calm and steady as a rock. He drove back to the cabin and we made it in fine shape, although the single vehicle we encountered on the logging road was not so lucky. The driver overreacted to our approach and rolled his truck up the side of the hill where it hovered momentarily, then rolled back down again, landing on its side in front of us.

Two heads popped out of the window, waved to signal they were OK, then asked us "if the fish were in yet." Leroy assured them they had hit it right and the run was in full swing, and while Gramps toasted their health the rest of us got out and helped roll their truck back up on its wheels. They headed off in a cyclonic cloud of Humboldt County steelhead dust.

Next morning I learned what a close call it had been for Leroy in the hotel bar. Just before midnight he had a serious argument with three Hoopa Indians. The argument centered around the question of who had better eyesight, whites or Indians, and things began heading rapidly in the wrong direction when one of the Hoopas pulled a knife. The Indian stood and asked Leroy if he could see that fly outside—"the one sitting on the telephone pole, just under the street lamp"—while he pointed at it with a ten-inch steel blade. The Indian spoke loudly and all the other patrons heard him; my father said the bar suddenly got as quiet as a church and everyone thought Leroy was a dead man. In fact, everybody in the bar, drunk or sober (but mostly drunk), rotated on their stools to watch the Indian. He had the knife in one hand, pointing toward the window, while his other hand clenched Leroy's sweat-soaked collar.

Leroy swallowed hard, looked the Indian right in the eye, and said: "No, I can't see the fly. But I can hear it fart." With that, a great cheer erupted from the crowd. Everyone jumped to their feet, applauding Leroy, stomping, pounding empty glasses on the bar and yelling for more. The Indian put his knife back in its sheath, ordered another round of doubles, then sat down and slapped his new friend Leroy on the back. He invited Leroy and his friends to his cabin after the bar closed, but Gramps smiled and politely declined on Leroy's behalf.

"We gotta get up early," he said. "'Goin' sshteeelheadin'."

That was the truth, at least where I was concerned. For the next three days I fished an hour or two each morning, flogging the same pool with the same spinner and the same disappointing results. Nobody else fished. My father spent the time working on his new mining claim while Leroy and Gramps went hunting for Big Foot with the .38. Each afternoon all three returned to the bar at the Orleans Hotel while I waited outside in the station wagon.

After several days of this it dawned on me that Gramps and Leroy would never find any gold or catch any steelhead and in truth the only reason they went to the Klamath was for the chance to meet Darlene. So far she still hadn't shown up, but Leroy insisted it was just a matter of time and we made plans for a return trip in late October.

As it happened, that October trip was the last time I ever saw Leroy or Gramps. We returned to the Klamath late in the month and I finally caught a steelhead, my first one, on the spinner. I held the little fish—it couldn't have been more than seven inches long—in the palm of my hand and examined it closely. It was spotted like a little wet leopard, with an olive back and two brave, innocent eyes. Each flank had a row of little lavender moons, the marks of a steelhead parr, and each small cheek wore a light blush of pink. Its belly was pure white and each scale was a perfect diamond. When I rotated the fish in my palm it sparkled like a rainbow.

I held it just long enough to memorize every detail. It was more beautiful than I could possibly have imagined, and I wondered what such a fish would be like when it returned to the river after two years in the ocean. I released it and watched as it slipped from my fingers and disappeared in the gravel of the river bottom.

But it didn't stop there. That night I saw it in the sea, where it swam beneath great waves of moonlight and blue caps of polar ice, always knowing the way back to the place where I had hooked it. After that I was never the same, and I promised myself that, like the fish, I would someday return to the Klamath. At the time I didn't fully realize all the implications of that promise. I guess you never do.

Seasons passed, each into the other. Then one day a few years later, as I passed the village of Happy Camp on my way to go steelhead fishing, I happened to look down at the river. Half a mile below, the Klamath formed a long, beautiful pool in the shape of an Indian bow. The sun was setting and a veil of soft orange light illuminated the hillside across the river. The riffle at the top of the pool was triangular in shape, an arrowhead of choppy current studded with boulders. I looked downstream just in time to see a fish jump in the tail of the pool. Then another fish showed, just a few feet upstream, followed in rapid succession by two more.

I pulled over to the side of the road, got my rod out of the back of the truck and hiked down to the river. Nobody else was around and there were no other vehicles on the road above. My hands trembled as I waded into the pool and removed my fly from its perch in the cork rod handle. The fly was a nameless cross between the Silver Hilton, an old Klamath standard, and a Canadian Kamloops pattern called the Doc Spratley.

Even now, years later, I can see the rod and the way the light ran up the chocolate-colored shaft as the bastard hairwing pattern sank into the foam and bubbles. The pull came almost instantly. The Winston bowed to the water and my first steelhead on a fly turned away violently and fled downriver as if it could part the waters by sheer strength. Seconds later it stopped behind a boulder with both our lives on the wire, his running into mine through this strange and wonderful connection we call fishing.

The fish jumped so many times I lost count before it came finally to my grasp. Its eyes bore into mine as I picked up a heavy stone and killed it, leaving me with feelings I cannot adequately describe. I made a pool inside a circle of rocks, laid the fish on its side and covered it with branches just in case a motorist stopped on the road and decided to look through a pair of binoculars. I didn't want any company or competition.

The second fish came from the center of the pool after a long cast toward the far side; it was a twin of the first and I kept it, too, placing it next to its brother in the funeral cage of stones and twigs.

The third steelhead was lying in the tailout, only a couple of feet above the roar of rapids. She took the swinging fly near the end of the drift with a violent yank that tied me in knots. She, too, was added to my catch. I cut a forked stick from a willow sapling, shaved off the leaves and twigs, and threaded the sticks through the gill rakers of the three trout so that twenty pounds of fresh Klamath steelhead hung from the branch like silver ornaments on a tree.

When I looked up again the sun was almost gone and the Klamath was pouring darkly through mountain shadows, tinted emerald green by trees along its banks. The shallows reflected the sunset like hammered gold, glittering with the last light of day. Insects flew in the light like orange comets with fluorescent tails.

I had done it. Here I was, standing in the river with three of the largest Klamath steelhead anyone could hope to catch. I turned and looked up the dark ravine. The trail was no longer visible, just the forest reaching out over the tunnel that led back to my truck. I headed for the spot full of emotion and youthful pride. Those were the last steelhead I ever killed on purpose.

For several years after that I lived in the northern California college town of Chico. I chased striped bass at night and chinook salmon, steelhead, resident rainbow, brown trout and bass by day—not to mention the occasional co-ed. Most of the co-eds would have little to do with me, however—possibly because I was beginning to look less and less like a student myself. Or maybe it was the music; I could no longer understand it, or tolerate it: "Oon dang tang rhang rhang bing bang, now I know you wanna hang . . . by my side and be the airplane of my mind but baby I don't have the time, your motor's down and I'm the other side of town so our love just can't grow, oon dang tang."

I finally gave up and started chasing girls with boots who could run a plow.

It was autumn of 1974 before I returned once more to the Klamath. I left Chico late in the morning, passed Redding about noon, and pressed on steadily before deciding to stop in Weitchpec to buy a fishing license and get gas. The town finally appeared over the hood of my truck and slid up the windshield as I pulled over at a dry-goods store. The wooden sign in front of the store had an addendum trimmed in green and nailed in place: "Fishing Tackle and Bait." The store itself was in a poor location on a side street and needed paint.

The front door had a bell; those kinds of stores always do. The bell jingled as I entered and I saw several boxes of flies sitting on a worn glass counter. I went over to take a look; the flies included a few Klamath patterns but nothing special, and nothing I needed. An old steelhead mount grimaced from the back wall. When it was alive it had been a good fish, a Klamath male of about seven pounds.

I could feel the fever rising. The run was in. I knew it. There was nobody behind the counter, or elsewhere in the store. I glanced at my watch, inspected the boxes of flies a second time, looked at some tools, renewed acquaintance with the grimacing steelhead, then looked at my watch again. I was still alone.

Then I saw her. She walked into the store as if by magic, barely touching the floor, floating through the curtains that screened the living quarters in the back. She was beautiful, extraordinarily so, with long, shiny hair as black as coal, and cathedral eyes of amber and white. She wore a loose-fitting blouse embroidered with coiled stitches of pink thread and four buttons of fake pearl. She smiled. A real smile. Then she winked. A real wink.

I recognized her gaze: the one of ten thousand nights. That one. Where do they learn that? Her face lit up, becoming more beautiful. Pale shoulders lifted elegantly from her blouse like the wings of a dove about to fly away. Cowboy boots clicked on the old wooden floor. Faded Levis were wrapped tightly around her hips and her tooled leather belt with silver buckle drew the line almost too late, pressing well below her navel. Her waist was as tiny as a wasp's, her legs long, slender and tapered.

It was instantaneous and inevitable. She was mesmerizing and I wanted her. In plain language I wanted to get her pregnant right then and there, down on the floor next to the brooms and mops. I wanted to throw away the key and crawl all over her every night until I was so old I had no teeth and she'd have to sneak out the window at night to meet the paper boy. I couldn't help myself.

At first she said nothing. She just looked at me. A bad sign? A good one? Who knew? I considered strategies. How many and what kind of promises would it take? How many fly rods or reels? I even considered giving up my E.C. Powell seven-footer, rarest of the rare, or any of my antique Hardys. How much cash, how many diamond rings, lacquered red Ferraris or tennis racquets would be required?

She smiled again, showing just the tip of her tongue. She liked me! Who would believe it? But what could possibly come of this? After all, I was only a fisherman; even worse, I was a wet-fly fisherman, crude and uncivilized. I used spit for fly sink and preferred Woolly Buggers to Hendricksons or Quill Gordons.

But she: She was a Goddess. She was perfect. I couldn't bear the thought of losing her. Was this all just a dream? It was indeed almost beyond belief. After a single Coca Cola and one of the most pleasant conversations I ever had with anyone, male or female, she was next to me on the warm leather seat of my rusty 1957 Chevrolet pickup truck and we were headed for the Klamath River. Without a fishing license.

The day was warm and yellow, the mountains shining. Waylon Jennings crooned his best through the chrome grill of the radio and when I pulled off the main highway onto a dusty logging road I could scarcely believe my eyes as she started to undress.

Her boots went first, disappearing effortlessly beneath the seat. Each button of her silky blouse dissolved with a touch of a red nail and slender finger. She looked over at me and smiled, her mouth watery and wet as the blouse fell from those beautifully carved ivory and alabaster shoulders.

I shifted gears, going from third to second, missing the double clutch, almost dropping the tranny, but what difference would it make? Waylon seemed to agree, changing chords on his guitar. The Klamath roared in the distance and we turned south, bouncing along parallel ruts through thickets of manzanita and pine. She shifted in her seat and adjusted the volume, making Waylon louder.

Maybe she just wants to dance, I thought, searching my pockets for cigarettes that weren't there. Oh God, now what? For a moment I considered smoking the steering wheel as she leaned back near the open window, inhaling clean mountain air, still smiling, dangling one long slender arm out of the window like a wand. Rainbows circled my eyes; a storm was gathering. I could smell the rain. Her long black hair trailed in the wind and she arched her back, the way women sometimes do, and exhaled softly. The light ran down her skin and suddenly I knew. Her name was Darlene. It was her. It had to be. I asked and she nodded yes. I asked her last name and she leaned forward, put her arm around me and whispered softly, "Oh, honey, what does it matter? I hear you're quite a fly tyer. Why don't you tell me all about it?"

The drummer came in with a roll and Jennings went into the last stabbing chorus as I started with the first thing I could think of—dubbing with synthetics as opposed to natural fur. She leaned against the door panel, listening, and then, just as I was about to get into dubbing loops, she uncoiled like a panther, arched her back again, and the Gates of Eden opened in front of me: the leather belt and tooled silver buckle came unhinged from her waist, something snapped (probably my mind), and the tiny brass handle of her zipper descended. Hooked thumbs pushed denim past the point of no return.

It was now 2:25 and I was doing seventy-three in third gear. Willie Nelson replaced Waylon Jennings on the radio and I switched from synthetics to natural furs as everything she was wearing fell to the floor and damn near burned through the bottom of the truck. There she sat, as white as snow and just as naked, squirming restlessly on the leather seat while Willie did his thing and I drove on, trying to remember my name and the part about how you take the dubbing and twirl it in your fingers. In little circles. The slower, the better.

When we reached the riverbank, I considered the possibility that the afternoon bite might be on, that perhaps a fish would roll, one willing to take a fly, and I looked at my fly box, then at the pool in front of us while she stood there pushing her toes into the mud. But I looked only for a second and with my eyes closed, and sure enough nothing rolled. I closed the fly box and reopened my eyes.

Now I never tell anyone how I take off my clothes. I'm too shy, and besides, it isn't proper etiquette. Anyway, I don't even remember how I did it that afternoon. I think they just dissolved as we hit the water.

The river was spectacular, filled with yellow sunshine and riffles like bouncing lace. She entered the stream on her stomach, a gleaming tadpole wiggling over slimy rocks and through puddles of warm water that felt like soup. I followed and our arms and legs churned up sand and bubbles as we headed for the center of the river.

When we reached the far side of the river she climbed up on a warm, sunny rock and I pulled up alongside, dumbfounded and mesmerized. Water fell like rain from the tips of her toes and fingers, dropping softly down to earth in slow motion, soaking into the moss and sand until I was ready to get on my hands and knees and lick the very ground where she stood.

No wonder. I was falling in love. Shameless love. Howling love. The love of wolves. No wonder Leroy and Gramps and all the others had caught the fever when they saw her. Who could resist?

We drifted downriver together, eye to eye, arms and legs wrapped around one another. It was only three o'clock Saturday afternoon, not even close to dark, and I had won the lottery. What were all those poor bastards in the Orleans Hotel bar doing at this very moment? Getting drunk for nothing. Too bad, boys.

Darlene and I kept paddling. We held hands like a couple of kids, floating on our stomachs, her heart beating into mine as we drifted downstream with our faces submerged, peering into deep underwater canyons and grottoes, now and then glimpsing a chinook or steelhead, suspended in the water beneath us, turning and drifting with us.

It was, as they say, perfect.

It was dark by the time we walked back upstream to the truck. I offered to build a fire but she merely smiled and held her hand over the earth as if to say, "No, I'll do that."

Somewhere out in the dark river a salmon broached and I could feel the river rolling over my back and his. I trembled; the fever grew. She said nothing and built the fire, a perfect blaze on the first attempt, without gasoline, paper or much of anything to get it going as far as I could tell.

Then suddenly, from out of nowhere it began, somehow, to rain. How could this be? A few moments earlier we had been looking up at stars.

Her fingers were electric and lightning crackled as she raised her hands to the sky. Her belly rolled, then receded. Somehow, suddenly we were in the dirt, all wrapped up in a mess of tangled hair, sweat and warm mud.

I can't say much about what happened next because I promised her I wouldn't, but later we went for another swim and afterward we returned to the fire. There she showed me how to make a hollow in my stomach. She filled the hollow with water dipped from the river, knelt and drank like a cat while her shining black hair tumbled down over me.

And, as I recall I persevered all night, an extraordinary feat I am still quite proud of. But I knew it would end; it had to.

I think she sensed it, too. Time was running out. It would soon be daylight. The last salmon porpoised with a splash and the moon began to fade.

Then she rolled on her back, smiled up at me, and said, "I will now teach you the final secret," a mystery she said she had never shared with anyone. Looking up at a swirling galaxy of stars, with the light swelling in her eyes, her long hair spread in a perfect fan along the river's edge, she pressed her stomach and breasts to me for the last time. Her breath came in a cloud of mist in my ear and I heard something incredible: She told me she could make rainbow trout leave their watery homes upon her command and, miracle of miracles, come leaping for her, and I watched as trout broke the surface like a rain of magic arrows. Her stomach heaved again; the bones in her hips curled around me. I could smell her; she was like the earth, like water, like every river I had ever fished, like the morning rain I have tasted on autumn leaves when no one was looking.

How could she know such a thing? The trout didn't answer; they merely vaulted into the air and turned somersaults for her, then slipped smoothly back into the black pool and swam in circles until she snapped her fingers. Then, as suddenly as they had appeared, they were gone.

I had never seen such a thing, or even thought of it. I asked her if salmon or brown trout or bass could do the same. She smiled, looked me in the eye, ran her tongue around the edge of her mouth, put her arms around me, and whispered in my ear: "No, they can't. But you can, can't you?"

After that I slept, and when I finally awoke she was still there, standing in front of me, behind the counter in the store in Weitchpec, next to the fly boxes and beneath the grimace of an old and weathered steelhead still glued to the board.

How much time had passed since I entered the store? Had I said anything during my reverie? Did she have any idea what had just happened? I looked at the floor; it was dry, without evidence of even a single drop of water. I hadn't been anywhere except in my own mind. Shit.

"Are you all right?" she asked. "May I help you?"

I stammered and stuttered, barely getting the words out. "I, uh, I, uh, need a license, a one year's fishing license, fresh water, for trout and steelhead, that's it. Thank you, Miss."

She turned and opened a drawer, extracted the necessary form, and handed it to me.

"Fill this out," she said. "I'll be right back."

I watched as she moved to the rear of the store. A drinking fountain was mounted on the wall next to a stack of old newspapers and a Coca-Cola vending machine and I thought I'd die when she bent over and took a drink, but I did as I was told.

When she returned I was finished and gave her the form. She leaned over the counter, purposely revealing the architecture of an impeccable bosom. Free from any undergarments, she strained against the fabric. The Pyramids of Egypt, the milky crest of Everest and the arc of a curving fly rod would never be the same. All withered in hopeless, awkward comparison.

I memorized almost everything I saw, even the discreet, very small tattoo, until I felt myself running out of air. Then I looked away, seeking refuge for my eyes, and noticed a duck calendar—one with the usual picture of a flock of mallards flying over a pond. I looked closer; the calendar was two years out of date.

To hell with time, I thought. This was my opportunity, that's what time it was, and that was all that mattered. I looked back at her. The moment of truth. Do or die. She smiled again and handed me my license.

I was just about to say something, the most clever and poetic thing I could think of, something about the essence of life and how I knew the deepest desires and secrets of women. I was about to tell her we could go together to the Klamath and I would show her how to swim the river, how to drink water from the leaves, how to catch steelhead on the fly.

I would tell her I was in the fishing business myself, that I knew Mike Fong, Andy Puyans, John Randolph, Bill Schaadt and Mel Krieger. What more could she want? I even had a fly shop of my own, with all the right stuff—Metz capes, including natural blue dun, Leonard bamboo rods, Fin-Nor reels, and 20,000 Mustad 94840s in assorted sizes. She could have it all, even my '57 Chevy.

But it was not to be. At that very moment a large, burly man plowed through the curtains like an ugly bear that somehow had learned to hold a can of beer and walk and talk at the same time. He was drunk and scowled at me. "Hey," he said, "everything OK in here?"

"Yes, John," she replied, "'Everything is fine. He just got a license."

"Well then, get back in here, goddammit!" he rumbled, and disappeared back behind the curtains.

I was ready for anything except what happened next: She turned away without a word—no sign, nothing at all—and followed the bear through the curtains. No diamond droplets of water fell from her fingers, no images of rainbow trout leapt in the moonlight, no trace of Klamath River mud could be seen in her shining hair. Only her eyes still seemed watery and wet. They were the last things I remember. I never saw her again.

I haven't fished the Klamath River since. My father kept his mining claim for a few more years, and I went back there with him once or twice to help with the work, but in the end we found no gold and finally let the claim lapse.

As for Darlene, I heard that she still occasionally appeared in the bar at the Orleans Hotel and still refused to have anything to do with Leroy, although she smiled twice at Gramps. We learned that much in a letter from Leroy, who was man enough to admit the truth. I guess that was also about the time he gave up fishing for steelhead in the Klamath or anywhere else, which was too bad.

Gramps made his last trip to the Klamath sometime in the late 1970s. He finally drank his last toast in a quiet space between hard October rains. I considered going to his funeral and leaving a small jug in his coffin, just to keep him company along the way, but thought better of it.

Now people say the fishing in the Klamath is good again, but I don't think so. The kind of fishing I remember happened a long time ago. I don't think we'll ever see its like again.

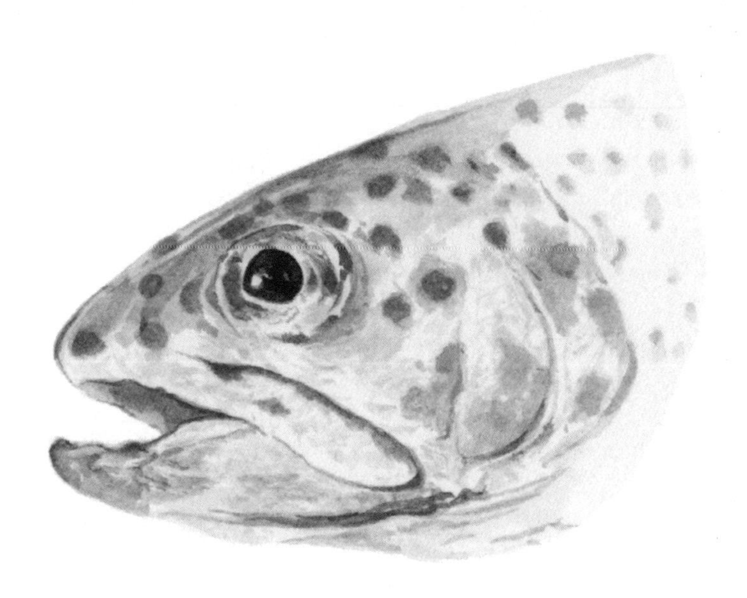

One Day on Fred Burr Creek

It's no accident Montana is the place most American anglers dream of plunking their Egg-Sucking Leeches or Quill Gordons. If your neighbor has a fly rod and you ask him where to go fishing, chances are he will tell you about the Madison, the Jefferson or the Big Hole.

Montana has everything (with all due apologies to the Battenkill): monster trout, fishing fantasies, Big Sky. It's the Super Bowl of American trout fishing. Norman MacLean's novella, *A River Runs Through It*, sealed the deal forever, and now Montana trout swim in our heads—hook-jawed browns with red lantern spots and brookies so fat they look like sides of Canadian bacon. But rainbows are the most beautiful of all and everyone knows it. There are lots of rainbows in Montana and always will be, with or without whirling disease.

I first found them in 1957 while nosing around the Madison, Gibbon and Firehole. I was fishing with a guy named Nick Zydycrn and he was a better angler than I was, although I managed to confuse the issue with lots of angling rhetoric even more complicated than the spelling of his name. Nick always kept his nose to the water, and one day he found a small tributary of the Firehole we called No-

Name Creek. No-Name was a covered artery pouring into the Firehole through deep undercut banks and a tunnel of grass, its mouth completely hidden. You had to know it was there. It ran consistently at fifty degrees, much cooler than the steamy temperature of the main river in August.

One day while Nick was floating hoppers on the Firehole a few yards away, I counted twenty trout lying in the mouth of No-Name. The biggest rainbow was more than five pounds and one of the browns looked as if it was pushing eight. I didn't catch either one, but it was a great moment when both moved forward a foot or so just for a better look at my brown nymph before they rejected it. I could hear trumpets.

Three years later my parents bought property on Montana's Fred Burr Creek. Few people have heard of Fred Burr because it isn't very important. It's small, too brushy for casting, has no fly-fishing status and is a long way from your typical Montana Blue Ribbon trout stream.

Our family built a fishing cabin on Fred Burr and we often spent our summer vacations there. As the cabin took shape, my mother always steadfastly refused my offers to take her fly fishing at the end of the work day because I was a snob about my fishing when I was young, and I was too competitive. Even my father was afraid of jumping into the stew.

"Besides, you don't catch enough that way," she said, gesturing at my fly rod and leather-trimmed wicker creel which often came home lighter than I liked. She, on the other hand, was a killer with four-pound monofilament and a piece of worm skewered on a talon-shaped Eagle Claw hook. I knew I'd never be able to keep up with her if we fished on her terms; yet I was anxious to show her something about trout. I also thought I might have a chance to talk with her in the bargain.

I was twenty-three at the time, with no orthodox future in sight—certainly not the kind my parents wanted me to have—and I knew that if we were going to go fishing together, and I was going to try to explain myself to her in the process, I would have to do it her way. The thought was paralyzing.

That was forty years ago, but I still remember that day—the smell of the air and the dust we stirred walking along the road to the stream. We had agreed to compromise: I carried a tin can of yellow corn and she carried the can opener.

Fred Burr was still cloaked in morning shade when we arrived. There was an overhanging shelf of green grass on the far side, good hopper water, but I didn't have any Joe's Hoppers—that was part of the compromise. As we found a place to sit next to the stream I smelled my mother's perfume. She never wore much, but I knew her warmth and scent nevertheless. I was nervous. We were so close we were almost touching.

I smiled at her, one of those polite family smiles you use just to show you care but one that reveals little else. I still didn't really know what it meant to be her son. What are sons supposed to do? I had always done my best, but I knew it was something less than perfect. Here I was in my twenties, scaring her to death riding freight trains across country and running around with women of doubtful but intoxicating reputation while barely scraping through a college education for which she and my father had sacrificed much. I had two decent shirts, six girl friends, twenty fly rods, 3,000 miles in a box car and a single pair of Levis to my name. My grade-point average hovered near 2.0—a miracle, considering what little time I spent in class or studying. I had Double Probation stenciled on my forehead.

And I had to do something about it. Maybe a day of fishing on Fred Burr Creek might offer a chance to tell her that I had decided to leave the halls of higher education and find a more comfortable venue to think about my future—like maybe hitchhiking to South America to see my friend Nick, who was then teaching in the steamy barrios of Guayaquil, Ecuador. After that I would go to Europe. Spain, I had heard, was interesting; the Mediterranean coastal resort towns were reportedly inexpensive and inhabited by European beauties in string Bikinis who gathered each summer to spawn and listen to Mick Jagger pouring his tonsils out in the discos.

Montana water is smooth in the morning because the wind usually doesn't come up until afternoon, and I had hoped to begin our fishing with a demonstration sensitive enough to throw her off guard. I'd show her how to look at the mirror-like surface of a pool and see the clouds in it. Then, as it became lighter, it would be simple to teach her how to look both at the surface and through it simultaneously, so she could see the trout swimming down below. I wanted her to see a whole pool full of hungry rainbow trout swimming around with bullets of corn in their mouths. Then, at the apex of her excitement, I would introduce my plan and deliver my final argument.

We sat next to the creek for a while and talked about school, my father, my brother and sister, my aunts and uncles, and about our cabin and how we could make it better. She was sewing some new curtains for the cabin, she said, and would put them up as soon as they were finished.

Twenty minutes passed. No breeze came, only the sound of hoppers clicking in the grass as their legs warmed. I heard a jay calling somewhere behind us, its voice flaring, then trailing off into nothing. As if the jay had said it was safe to do so, a trout suddenly appeared near a stone in the center of the pool. A few small mayflies began to emerge and my mother and I sat still and watched as the trout began to feed.

A second trout swam cautiously in view, followed moments later by a third and then a fourth, each emerging from the shade beneath the grassy overhanging bank. I could see their eyes sweeping the bottom of the pool as they cruised, looking for something to eat. Now and then one would rise suddenly to the surface and circle around a floating twig or a mayfly, then dive back to the bottom like a submarine. My mother leaned forward, watching intently. I'm not sure she had ever seen that before.

Another fifteen minutes went by and the creek turned yellow in the rising sun. Only the far bank remained in shadow, a narrow ribbon of shade. I knew fish were in the shade. A lot of them. I opened the can of corn.

"Will they really eat that?" she asked.

"Oh, yeah, Mom," I said. "Trout love corn."

"How do they know what it is?"

"I'm not sure. They just do, that's all."

"Do you think you should get a haircut? It's getting pretty long, and your father is worried and your Uncle Bill even thinks you might be, well, you know, different or something, but I know better than that. Maybe you should marry. Someone like Rachael. That would show everyone. Remember her? Such a nice girl. She sang in the church choir."

I didn't know how to respond to any of that. I visualized Rachael in her usual position behind the mahogany banister at church. She always sat in the third row of the choir, her eyes focused on the hymnal, surrounded by varnished oak and Lutheran mysticism, unreachable. She was honest and well-intentioned—a solid girl that I did not know how to talk to or touch. I would ruin her with my smoking, my vulgarity, my obsession with fishing and, one day perhaps, with the scent of perfume on my clothes when I came home too late at night for any excuse. I wasn't ready and in any event the relationship would be hopeless.

The first kernel of corn pierced the surface of the pool and my mother watched it sink. It gleamed like a gold nugget.

A pair of eyes appeared from under the shadowy bank. This was a bigger fish, perhaps a pound or so. I held my breath. The trout cocked its head, taking the scent, then rushed to the corn like a bonefish on shrimp. The kernel disappeared in its mouth and my mother's eyes grew large.

Corn fell in a golden rain. Trout came as if from nowhere. Soon the entire pool was filled with rainbows, feeding ever more aggressively. Some took the corn on the run as soon as a kernel hit the water. Others fed on the bottom like carp. Larger fish chased away smaller companions trying for a share of the feast. Still others waited like trained seals, sipping each piece as it fell to the surface.

I looked at my mother. She was smiling.

She had been right about one thing: I have often mused about the differing psychologies of men and women, and although I never had any doubts about which one I wanted to be, I do find the differences intriguing. Men are mysterious—the planners, the clever thinkers. They build complicated devices, worry about the size of their genitals and become serial killers; they collect property and anything else they desire while planning the next war and their eventual domination of outer space and the world corporate environment. The worst of them consider the earth as a subsidiary.

On the other hand, women are not mysterious, contrary to the popular belief of men. All you have to do is look to see the evidence. Women go for the heart, sometimes for better and sometimes for worse, and carry the tools of their trade in their eyes. They are not only our best temptation, but our best hope. It's true some worry about the shape or size of their breasts, but it was men who put them up to that. The rest of the package either escapes me or is of little interest, except for one thing: Women, along with fishing, offer the only consistent, benevolent and tolerable form of relief a man has from the raging storms of his own mind. Or so it seems to me.

For some, Rachael would be perfect. And I might be one of them, I thought.

But I had never really known my mother—not completely, not thoroughly, not as a friend. Saddest of all, there were times when I felt too distant to be her son. I never knew why. Maybe there wasn't any reason. Maybe that's just the way it is sometimes, and nobody is to blame.

I think she knew what was going on in my mind, because when the jay called again she turned and looked at me from a vantage point I could barely understand. Her eyes held light—the light of her age and all the years spent doing everything she could for her family, most of all the honesty of her labor. She was tied to all of us by that and her caring, which went beyond anything I could understand. I couldn't match her gaze.

I looked at her fingers as she reached for the can. They were plain and beautiful; no nail polish, no vanity, no lace or nylon at the cuff, just the rolled-up sleeve of a faded cotton fishing shirt.

Time ran backward in a drifting balloon, past the blue veins of her wrist, past the afternoon she came to watch me play ball in high school, past the image of her working in the cafeteria just to pay for the clothes I wore, beyond her graying hair and all the way back to the Missouri fields where she grew up. It all stopped with the biggest heart I could imagine.

What could I possibly teach her? She was my mother. And I cursed myself that morning on Fred Burr Creek because I could feel the time coming for her and couldn't bear the thought that someday she would die. She was simply too important.

I stood there like an idiot, clearing my throat and trying to look indifferent. She was the most unselfish, uncomplicated person I've ever known, yet I was falling apart while she stood on her toes, tossing corn to the trout.

Finally I told her my plans. She said nothing, but I knew she sensed the danger and uncertainty of those plans even without hearing all the details.

Just before dark we started back to the cabin and I noticed she had taken off her shoes to walk barefoot on the dusty road.

"I always used to do this on the farm when I was a little girl," she said softly. "It's OK, isn't it?"

I nodded and told her I loved her without saying the words. They came from the way I turned my head and looked at her, I guess, but I think she understood.

I never fished alone with her after that, but the following Christmas she smiled when she opened the smallest package under the tree. It was a box of hooks I had given her—100 size 14 gold-plated Mustads, short shanked, light wire. Perfect for fishing with corn and she knew it.

I left for Panama the following week.

During the last days of her life I went home many times to see her and managed to get in some fishing during my visits. After visiting her, I'd leave the hospital and drive hard in the old truck, almost to the edge of the river. I had a favorite gravel bar on the Sacramento River, not far from the hospital where she was confined. Striped bass run up the Sacramento in the spring and if you're quiet you can see them in the evening, rolling and pushing through the shallow riffles as they search for deeper water in which to spawn.

Sometimes another angler would be there, but usually the others never stayed long. They were after shad and knew nothing about stripers. They would quit when it got dark, not knowing that sometimes the moonlight would produce just enough glare on the surface so you could see the triangular push and swell of a bass swimming upstream.

But most of the time I fished alone in darkness without much to go on. I would think about her then, while I cast repeatedly in an empty, ritualistic way, over a river I couldn't see.

Death makes you lighter and as she came closer to it, she slowly grew more and more like that until it seemed she was not in her bed but above it, almost floating. Late one afternoon, near the end, I went to see her, trading the outside sounds of summer crickets for the steady hum of medical electricity inside the hospital.

She was asleep and I didn't wake her, although I wanted to. Instead, I turned silently and went back out into the warm Sacramento Valley air. I got in the truck and headed out of town, driving until it was night and the headlights brought life to the gnarled stumps and twisted trees along the road. It seemed as if I was driving backward in time. When I finally reached the river I felt like I was only six years old.

I took my fly rod from the back of the truck and a wallet full of bushy black flies from the dashboard and headed for the river. A bright corridor of moonlight stretched across the pool and I knew it would reveal the surge of water passing over the dorsals of striped bass on their way upstream. I fished alone that night as man and boy, beneath a soft yellow moon that slipped ever farther from my sight. I made my last cast just before dawn with eyes full of tears at the image of my mother in a gothic wrap of white linen. She floated before me, isolated in time and space, with my casts going through her and the swimming fly moving in currents so deep I was afraid I would never find the end of them.

She died a week later, carried away by a howling wind and the fire of her cremation in a ceremony that broke my heart.

Seedling Creek: Confessions of an Ex-Hippy

The night before my first assault on the waters of Seedling Creek I lay in bed thinking about Diane. She was somewhere on the Mediterranean and I imagined her with a lover she had just met, a man with broad shoulders, curly black hair, big muscles and legs like a thoroughbred horse. I, on the other hand, had boring brown hair and was skinny. The comparison kept me awake even though I was high at the time. I wasn't high quite as often as I led everyone to believe, although in those days I did inhale. More than once.

That night, when I inhaled, I could visualize Diane draped in the arms of her lover, a Spanish sun at her back, her lips parted, the warm sea dripping from her limbs, and I really couldn't blame the guy. To hell with him, I thought; he had probably found the secret spot.

It had been an impossible situation from the beginning. I had fallen in love with her on a Thursday afternoon in the school cafeteria. When I invited her to sit down I couldn't look into her eyes without imagining the two of us in a sweaty embrace, and I was so nervous I dropped blueberry pie in my lap. When the pie landed she made a small red circle with her mouth, then politely covered it with her fingers. Her nails were long and painted red and I knew I was in for it.

"No," she said when I asked if she had a boyfriend. "I belong to the wind." She didn't mention a recent ex-boyfriend named Tim Worthington whom she still adored.

I had indecent thoughts about her from the first, but never knew how to go about making them come true. Nevertheless, her father wasn't wrong when he told her to "stay away from him because he's a low-life ruffian, too vulgar and coarse for the likes of you." How did he know? She told me I had used the "F-word" in front of him at the wrong time. I always wondered what the right time would have been.

Now, forty years later, it doesn't matter. Maybe Diane is dead now, although I hope not. She was a decent girl and my first love, even if she still was in love with some guy named Tim Worthington.

And, there was a war on at the time. Posters nailed to telephone poles showed images of American soldiers soaking into the dark soil of Vietnam; the communications denounced the conflict, and invited everyone to the next rally. I hated the images and the guilt I felt because those guys were fighting and dying and I wasn't, even though I once thought I might. In the spring of 1961 I was refused for the draft by the Army Induction Center in Oakland, California, for being "morally unfit to serve" because of a past felony conviction for possession of stolen property taken during a fraternity prank.

I decided not to tell Diane, or her father about that.

Meanwhile, down in Dixie and a few other places, folks were still being shot or hanged for having the wrong color of skin, and neither I nor most anybody else knew what to do about it except pop open another beer and wait for the next broadcast.

It got worse. A lot worse. In 1962, Diane locked herself in the bathroom for three days to demonstrate her love for Tim and would open the door only when offered pizza and a beer. Two of my classmates committed suicide weeks apart, one on heroin and one with a Smith & Wesson he stuck in his mouth at a party. Rock stars in snakeskin pants became the flamboyant priests of a new order, howling sermons to the faithful who believed every word. The sermons were about sex, revolution and drugs, which somehow all got tangled up together.

In retrospect we were all naive, and if you want to know what any of this has to do with fishing—well, that's what I'm about to tell you.

The morning after that sleepless night spent fantasizing about Diane and her imaginary lover, I decided the answer to everything was to simply get rich. That should, I thought, solve everything, including my future father in law's misgivings about my vocabulary. According to my calculations, I could harvest a single crop of marijuana and realize a profit of $250,000 in only ten short months—depending, of course, on average daily temperatures, winter frosts and rainfall. After the harvest and some last-minute steelhead fishing, I would head for Mexico with Diane, my Rolling Stones albums, a master's degree in psychology and twelve pounds of resin-soaked tips wadded up someplace where the narcs would never find them. Far out.

But I couldn't do all this alone. I was too scared. I could imagine the prison guards—day after day, month after month for endless years, shoving the same old food in the same old scratched-up aluminum tray under the same door, until one day when I could scarcely walk any more their sons would say goodbye and exit through the big iron gates with a gold watch and some photos of the day the governor stopped by to say hello.

If I went to prison, I wanted some company.

My freshman roommate would never agree to participate in my scheme; so despite his potential to help finance the farm, I never asked him. Ted W., however, said he was in. Ted was quiet and shy with curly black hair and brooding, nervous eyes. He was an English major with a solid B average and liked jazz more than anything else, especially under the influence of a good smoke.

Dan S. was in, too, and would be the leader. He was also an English major, but hated jazz and all other forms of music except for that of Johann Sebastian Bach, which he considered was probably a mathematical message from outer space delivered through Johann's brain cells. When humans finally learned to merge calculus with Bach's harmonic patterns they would discover the universal code, the answers to everything, including what was going on in the Mekong Delta, the final exam in poly sci, and whether Sigma Gamma women wore undies or not.

It was hard to argue with Dan. He was articulate, good looking, had a 4.0 grade average and was a member of something called the "Mensa Society," a group of people with IQs well beyond my own. He also was in a position to provide the opportunity I needed to get back in the woods and do the illegal planting: He had a summer contract with the California Division of Forestry to work on something called the "Blister Rust Control Program." In simplest terms, this meant walking through the woods searching for gooseberry plants and digging them up (gooseberry plants are hosts to the blister rust parasite, which kills pine and spruce.) After a designated block of timber had been cleared of gooseberry plants, the U.S. Forest Service would come in and inspect the work. If you had removed all the plants, you were paid; if you hadn't, you weren't.

Dan also had transportation. He owned a rusted-out 1949 Plymouth pickup and could drive like hell. The pickup had a chrome-plated spotlight on the driver's side, a stick-shift four-on-the-floor transmission, and no brakes. "Piss on the brakes," Dan always said. "If you plan ahead, and understand effective downshifting and compression parameters, you don't need brakes."

Dan's younger brother, whose name I don't remember now, would be the fourth member of the party. He was an aspiring actor (I actually saw him on Gunsmoke many years later) with an unusually soft voice and an innocent laugh that rolled out of his mouth like water. He would turn red in the face and keep laughing long after everyone else had stopped. Since he was the youngest and strongest of us, he could also do most of the digging.

The fifth guy, Carrot, was more focused although somewhat strange. I remember he frequently rubbed himself too much in places you shouldn't and kept shifting his weight from one leg to the other. This happened most often when he was discussing religion, a connection lost on me although I suppose the pleasures of the soul are not necessarily separate from those of the body. I also suspected either a structural problem or maybe a drug overdose at a Jefferson Airplane concert, but never asked. He had green eyes and red hair, almost orange, that reminded me of a carrot, and I gave him that nickname. He claimed to be a Bhuddist, something Ted noted with disdain, but Dan agreed he should be a member of our group. "I see you're left-handed," Dan said.

"That's OK. You can dig next to Waller."

As part of the arrangement I agreed to dig next to Carrot and share some of the horticultural proceeds (ten percent) with Dan and his brother. We signed a private harvest agreement based on material Ted found in the I Ching and ratified it at a terrific keg party on the banks of the Sacramento River. Everything was set: Dan and his brother would get a percentage of the profits while Ted and Carrot would dig with us but have nothing to do with the planting. It was too risky, they claimed.

All five of us would go for the forestry job, a summer of honest employment camping out on the meadowed banks of Seedling Creek at a campground in Hum Bug Valley. The daily commute would be easy, a ten-minute trip across a meandering meadow section of the creek's best dry-fly pools, then down the mountain into dense forest and tangled clots of gooseberry, hundreds of acres of both. There would surely be enough open space for a thousand marijuana plants or more, and for a while I considered expanding my original plans. Finally I decided against it. There was no need to be greedy; after all, I was a hippy.

The plan was simple. As I walked through the woods killing gooseberries with my shovel, I would also carry a fly rod and hit a pool with a dry fly whenever we crossed the creek. Or maybe I'd use a nymph or streamer. They were kind of new then, and I thought of them as almost magical—all that scraggly fur, and everything. Just like Diane.

I'd also carry illegal germinated seeds in my pack and, when an appropriate location was found, I'd drop them into the rich soil and spring-laden hillsides. For two or three weeks after planting, the shoots would be too small to look like anything in particular and thus would escape detection by the Forest Service inspectors who came to look at our gooseberry extractions. Then, in mid to late August, I would return to harvest the bonanza. I hadn't yet figured out just how I'd do that, but I would. I was the new Johnny Appleseed, on the ground floor of a generation that would change the world.

I had the seeds, a couple thousand at least, all segregated by variety—Acapulco Gold, Panama Red, Chico Green and Turlock Terror hidden away carefully in the basement of the Kappa Kappa Tau fraternity house, inside a surrogate womb of terrycloth towels. I also had something to plant them in; Thelma, the amiable cook at the fraternity house, had innocently given me a hundred cardboard egg cartons. I only had to wet the towels and germination would begin. Once the plants sprouted, I would fill the pockets of the cartons with a little dirt, remove the sprouts from the towels and plant them carefully in the cartons. When each sprout was an inch-and-a-half tall, it would be removed from the egg carton and planted in a carefully selected secret location known only to me.

I was confident I had learned much from an earlier attempt. This time I would not overfertilize, a mistake that had cost me 1,500 plants from nitrogen burn during my junior year. This time I'd be mellow and do a little fishing as I planted. If all went well, at least a thousand plants would reach full maturity, soaring to the sky under the nurturing sun, well rooted in the rich soil of upper Seedling Creek, less than two hours from campus and Diane's apartment (by the way, just so you know, Seedling Creek isn't the stream's real name.)

Classes were out June 15th and the five of us left Chico State Teachers College and headed north. Late that afternoon we pulled off the pavement and Dan downshifted the pickup as we turned onto a pair of logging ruts. A half hour later, through a grove of groovy trees just ahead, we reached our home for the next two months—the Seedling Creek Hum Bug Valley Campground. Many of the campsites already were occupied and some of the campers looked oddly at our truck, our long hair and our funny pants.

We pulled into a spot near the creek and as the Plymouth coughed to a stop a trout porpoised softly in the stream, scattering light and water in a series of concentric circles that radiated gold. I had a momentary vision of Diane setting the table in our Acapulco hacienda. She was pregnant and happy. On the wall was a photo of her father with a very large mustache she had painted on his face.

In those days someone still cut firewood for public campgrounds and there it was, split neatly and stacked next to the fire pit. Sanitation facilities were to the right, back in the trees. Tall trunks of soaring pine and spruce provided shade, allowing a late-morning sleep. "I can't dig before 10:00 in the morning," Carrot said. "I have to meditate."

"Yeah, OK," Dan answered, "but the first thing we have to do is choose the place where we want to sleep." I waited until Carrot decided, then took the opposite side of the camp, lining my bed with clumps of pine needles to provide a make-shift mattress. No one else knew that trick and when they saw me doing it, I had to show them how and it took us another thirty minutes to gather enough pine needles for everyone. Except Carrot. His complexion became even redder as he blew up an L.L. Bean air mattress.

The remainder of our camp included my three-burner Coleman stove, which we set up on the picnic table, and a matching green lantern suspended from a tree limb. The finishing touch was five cases of beer that we submerged in cold water at the creek's edge.

Ted and I took care of that chore, and I saw a couple more trout rise while we were doing it. But my E.C. Powell remained in its tube; Dan still had to give us the lowdown on how everything would work for the next two months before there would be time for fishing or anything else.

We began by drawing straws for the cooking, dishwashing and fire-building rotations. Those tasks wouldn't be hard, Dan said, because we had only one skillet, one pot, five sets of utensils, a single coffee pot and ten gallons of kerosene to start fires and operate the Coleman appliances. We also had $500 worth of credit at the Hum Bug Valley store, and once a week Dan would take the Plymouth down the hill to restock our groceries.

For our first night, he said, we would have steak, tossed salad and a fresh lid of Turlock Terror. After dinner and three lids of the Turlock Terror, we voted to allot no more than $250 of our grocery-store credit for food and save the rest for beer. We'd smoke a lot and be frugal with our grocery list.

When darkness fell I realized I'd get no fishing that evening, and I sat with the others as Dan told us how to clear gooseberry plants. We would walk through the forest, about fifteen to twenty feet apart, and look for gooseberries as we marched, he said. When we found one the guy closest to the plant would dig it up. No arguing; that would be bourgeois and decadent. But in case an argument did break out he would come over and measure the distance from the plant to the persons on either side of it. The closest guy would dig.

Dan also explained that it wasn't the digging that could go wrong, for the roots pulled out easily enough if you dug correctly. The danger was in missing plants. "If we miss too many, we don't get paid," he reminded us. "It's a lot of work, but the pay is righteous, man. We get five hundred bucks an acre if our work passes inspection."

For the next two weeks we dug energetically and the work progressed fairly well. Gooseberry plants lay scattered and drying in the sun on about 500 acres of national forest and I felt good about it. I think we all did, in a way. It was solid conservation work.

I also felt good about the fact that, since I had drawn the first turn as cook, I was able to get off early and devote the last three hours of each day to fishing. The daily limit was fifteen trout of any size and I returned each evening with fifteen trout in my creel. After cleaning them I'd put them in the ice box and we'd have fresh trout for breakfast or dinner, or both.

Everyone was impressed by my apparent fishing skills, which at that time were rare among long-haired students—or short-haired ones, for that matter. Hardly anyone fly-fished then.

One night after dinner, Ted wanted to take a look at the fly rod. I told him how it was made. "Six pieces of bamboo, Ted," I said proudly. "All the way from China and glued together so well you can't see the seams."

"Far out," he replied. "That's far out, man"

"What part of China?" Carrot asked.

"The upper Yang-Tse valley," I replied, although I didn't really know and gave him the name of the only Chinese valley I could think of. "They grow up there with panda bears and some kind of gibbon."

"That's cool, brother."

Over the next four or five days our digging grew more intense, and it wasn't long before we went from blisters to callouses. After that no one needed gloves any more. I think we were actually getting into shape and feeling better for it.

Evening conversations were usually friendly, relaxed and animated. One night, after a particularly easy block of timber had been cleared, we finished our peanut-butter sandwiches in high spirits and celebrated by drinking thirty or forty beers, smoking a particularly smooth batch of Acapulco Gold, and having a good discussion about extraterrestrial life. Everyone agreed the current hysteria over the possibility of hostile invasion from outer space was in fact impossible, and we listened to Dan, who said his studies had revealed there were no nearby planets capable of supporting intelligent life as we knew it. Any visitors reaching our galaxy therefore would have to come from light years away, and any life form that could make such a trip would be so highly evolved that violence would no longer be an option.

"They can only be made of love," he said, smiling, as we passed the joint.

Only an hour earlier I had taken a rainbow of almost three pounds and lost a big brown on a size 12 Royal Wulff, right at dark. I estimated the brown was close to five pounds. It was possible. There were many fish of that size down in Seedling Creek canyon if you wanted to walk five miles to fish for them. Surely a few of them migrated up to the meadow section where we were camped; it only stood to reason.

I looked out over the meadow where deer were grazing. A few fawns stood with their mothers; they came every evening to forage in the meadow.

The fires of other camps sparkled in the summer evening and the stars were coming out. It was one hell of a good night. It was even better than that. It was too much, brother.

"Hey, you guys know something?" Carrot said. "This is the way men are supposed to live, isn't it? I don't give a shit if I flunked poly-sci."

"Did you?" Someone asked.

"Hey, how do I know? Maybe I did, maybe I didn't, but I wouldn't care if I did. This is too cool, man. Can you dig it? Look at these trees. Wow. What difference would it make if I did flunk?"

"None," someone else said. "None at all."

And so it continued, for two, maybe three more weeks, and I caught a few more pretty good-sized trout, although none as big as the three-pound rainbow or the even larger brown I had lost. But I began to notice the fish were getting harder to catch. Dry flies didn't work as well as they had when I'd started fishing the creek and I was relying more and more on nymphs, although I really didn't know what I was doing or exactly how to use them.

Like the feeding habits of trout, the affairs and behavior of men also can change unexpectedly and for no apparent reason. I should have known that.

One morning dawned unusually warm, then became hot, unbearably so, finally passing the 100-degree mark by early afternoon. It was too uncomfortable to keep digging, so we returned early to camp, rewarding ourselves for working nearly eighteen days without a break. We also were certain our first paycheck was waiting in Dan's post-office box at the Hum Bug Valley store, and around 4:00 Dan left for town to get it, pay our grocery bill and stock up on more groceries.

Ted and Carrot had consumed most of our last remaining beer as they dug that day, and by noon Ted was grumpy and started bugging Carrot. Somehow they got into an argument about the density of human excrement. How they got onto such a subject was beyond me; maybe it was because of the deer droppings we found now and then. Anyway, I listened but stayed out of it.

Carrot asserted that bad karma was a function of diet, action and sometimes thought, and since we had been eating meat for nearly a month, everything, including our waste materials, had become dense and foul. Or something like that.

Ted liked to argue. "Who do you think you are, Carrot?" he responded. "Real Bhuddists only eat fruit that has voluntarily dropped off the tree and wear masks so they don't inhale living organisms."

"You're crazy," Carrot said. "You're just making fun of me. How do you know that?"

Ted looked at me and took a big drag from his joint. "Ravi Shankar told me," he said, exhaling with a smile.

Meanwhile the temperature had soared to nearly 105 and Dan hadn't yet returned with our wages, let alone beer, groceries or a letter from Diane. Seedling Creek looked cold and pure, and Dan's brother was already in the water cooling off. He wore plaid swimming shorts and was reciting a poem as he smiled up at the sky. He was also an English major; they must do something to English majors to make them act that way.

"Brain manipulation," Carrot said.

"Bullshit. You're the one who's crazy," Ted said. He got up, staggered down to the river's edge and jumped into the pool. Carrot got up and followed, then stopped at the edge of the creek, his pink beer belly hanging down over green nylon shorts.

"You're full of it, Ted!" he yelled.

Ted just smiled.

Two days earlier a man, his wife and two young children had taken the campsite next to ours. They were nice people who always wished us good morning and smiled and waved when we returned from work in the afternoon. I think they liked us. At least at first.

Now they were sitting by the water's edge watching Ted dog-paddle to the center of the pool. We watched too until we remembered that Ted couldn't swim and had always been nervous around water. Nevertheless, somehow—perhaps through advanced inebriation—he had relaxed and was now floating naked in the pool while Carrot stood on the bank, still arguing.

Ted no longer responded. In fact, he had grown strangely silent. I didn't see how the family next to us could have missed his nude entry into the water, or for that matter how they could have failed to overhear the content of the conversation. Embarrassed, I hid behind a tree and watched carefully to see what would happen next.

In the next camp the woman's eyes were bulging in disbelief and her husband was standing at attention and trying to speak, but no words came. I turned back to the river just in time to see Ted's bare buttocks broach the surface in a rolling porpoise, then disappear. Resurfacing, he tread water like a hippo, closed his eyes, blew a little water from his nose, and rolled over again. Two globes of white flesh appeared as if a manatee had broached and Ted suddenly produced evidence to support his theory about the connection between karmic reality and the density of human waste. The evidence floated downstream right in front of our new neighbors.

Nobody said anything. Ted climbed out of the water, belched, flipped Carrot off, fell down in the dirt and started crawling toward his sleeping bag. Once there, he paused, looked at Carrot, growled like a dog, peed on all fours and finally passed out.

To my amazement we weren't shot in our sleep that night, but when we awoke next morning the next campsite was empty except for a note nailed to a tree facing our camp. "You may rest assured that what you did will not go unreported to the proper authorities," it said.

After that things got worse. Dan returned with no letter from Diane, no beer, no groceries and no more credit. Two days later we learned we had flunked every forestry inspection. Every one. The red rejection slips were in Dan's box at the Hum Bug Valley post office.

Nothing had passed. Not one lot. We were broke and out of food.

An inventory of our remaining supplies disclosed two boxes of Aunt Jemima pancake mix and a jar of jelly. I could always catch more trout, though it was becoming necessary to travel farther and farther downstream to find them, but everyone recoiled at the thought of eating any more fish no matter how I cooked them.

Meanwhile, I was getting nervous. The marijuana seedlings were growing fast. Some had taken root in the wet towels and attempts to extract them were hopeless; their fragile stems just broke off. I had to transfer them to the egg cartons or lose them.

"Goddammit, let's have a meeting or something, that's the least we can do," Carrot said. "It's all Ted's fault. He brought this whole thing down by what he did in front of those people. It's bad karma, man, and we have to get out of here, or we're history. We'll go to jail, that's where we'll go."

"Shut up," Ted said. "What in hell do you know about karma? You said you could adios Lyndon Johnson. What kind of crap is that?"

Dan's brother and I tried to keep the peace, but things were getting worse by the hour and we all knew it. Someone tried to start a fire but used too much gas. After we put out the resulting blaze that had spread to the picnic tables and nearby trees, we sat down for a tribal council.

"Listen," Dan said, "we have to think rationally about this. This is not the time to lose our edge to raw emotion. We have to . . ."

"Oh, the hell with everything!" Carrot interrupted with a shout. "Dan, you're the leader. You should have done a better job of planning. We should have had some extra money in the bank or something to carry us over in case we didn't pass a few of our lots. Now what do we do? To hell with this, I say. Maybe we better get out of here. Maybe we better go now."

We all turned to look at Dan. He sat stiffly, arching his neck as I'd never seen him do. His face was composed but his eyes were alive in the firelight and we all knew he had something in mind that would save the trip, our summer wages and maybe even our lives.

Finally he got to his feet and exclaimed: "I have it!"

"Well, what is it?" his brother asked. "What do you have, Dan? What in the hell can we do?"

"In the first place, I'm sure our last two lots will pass," Dan said. "They were really clean. We did a good job. Maybe our best. So, that's a thousand bucks. We have to stay here and keep working and wait for the two last lots to pass. Don't you see? We're in the groove now. We're grooving, man."

"What about food?" Ted asked. "We don't have any food."

Dan didn't say a word, merely raised himself to full attention, bent his left leg and rested his foot atop a rock, then pointed with one arm like George Washington on the shore of the Delaware. We looked and saw he was pointing at the deer grazing peacefully in the nearby meadow.

For a moment we were all silent. Then it sank in.

"Oh no, Dan," his brother said. "Not that. We can't do that. What about all these people in the other camps? God, we'll all end up in jail."

"Oh, fuck them," Dan replied. "Don't you see? This is war. What do they know about basic survival? Look at their tents. It looks like they're made of silk. And look at that skinny one over there—the one with the white apron and chef's hat, doing the funky barbecue. He wouldn't last ten minutes without a trip to the grocery store. Where will he be after the revolution? Nowhere, that's where."

Dan was on a roll now and had everyone's attention. "Listen up, guys," he said. "Carrot is right: Power to the people. This is how it really is and we can either live or die. This is life, all right, and I don't know about all of you, but I don't want to die and I'm sick and tired of eating trout. Who wouldn't be? It isn't right and it's against nature. Men need red meat. We'll do it at night when everyone is asleep. No one will know."

Dan turned to me. "Waller here used to hunt deer and he's a hell of a shot," he said. "He will do any necessary shooting."

The color drained from Carrot's face. "Shooting?" he said. "What do you mean, shooting?"

"Shut up, Carrot," Ted said. "You're a fruit!"

"OK, OK, stop it, you guys," Dan said. "Here's what we do. The plan is simple; the best ones always are." He outlined what he had in mind: We'd wait until 2:00 in the morning when all the other campers were asleep. Then Ted, Carrot and Dan's brother would keep a lookout while Dan and I quietly took the brakeless Plymouth up the hill beyond the meadow, popped the clutch and drove as fast as we could straight at the herd of feeding blacktail.

"By the time we hit the meadow we should be doing about sixty, maybe sixty-five or even seventy," Dan said. "I've done the calculations and it looks closer to seventy, but it all depends on traction. Our first option will be to hit one of the deer, but if we miss Waller will open up with the gun. From what he tells me he's one of the best. It will probably only take him one or two shots at the most. Isn't that right?" He looked at me for confirmation.

I once hit a half-inch rope wound around the trunk of a ponderosa with a Winchester lever-action .30-30 and buckhorn sights at fifty feet. Maybe I'd told Dan about that, the only good shot I ever made.

"Yeah, that's right," I whispered.

"Then we'll kill the lights, drop the deer in the back of the truck, throw a gunny sack over it and take the long way back to camp on the back road, away from the campground," Dan went on. "No one will see us and we'll skin it out before dawn and by the time everyone wakes up we'll be all done having venison steaks for breakfast. Waller also knows how to gut and skin a deer."

Carrot looked ready to vomit. "Dan, I . . . I don't know about this," he sputtered. "I . . . uh, I just don't know."

"You must see the deer for what they are," Dan said softly. "And no more."

"Well, what do you mean by that? Just what are they, Dan?"

Dan didn't answer, and we all turned to look at the deer. By this time there were as many as fifty blacktail feeding quietly in the meadow. I didn't see any bucks, but bucks are spooky and always show up last, so at the moment the herd consisted only of does and fawns. At least none of the fawns had spots.

By 2:00 in the morning the big ones would be out, I thought, and I might get lucky and hit a four-pointer or better. Wouldn't it be far out if I got a new state record?

Meanwhile other campers were firing up their barbecues in anticipation of the evening meal. Now and then a change of breeze brought the scent of roasting sirloins, hot dogs, or something that smelled like chicken in a pretty good wine sauce. Sometimes a camera flashed as amateur photographers captured images of the valley or their kids posing with the deer and the meadow in the background.

We turned again to Dan, still waiting for his answer to the question of what the deer really were.

"Food," he said finally, smiling. "Food. That's what they are. Now, goddammit, who's in and who's out? I need to know."

Precisely at that moment the breeze brought us the renewed scent of searing fillets. "For God's sake, let's kill just one," someone whispered. "What can that hurt? Look at how many are out there . . . sonofabitch!"

Everyone nodded in agreement, hopping up and down and toking hard on Chico Green. Ted stepped forward and offered his hand to Dan. "Right on, brother," he said. "You're right. That's a hell of a plan." Everyone applauded.

I wondered where the bucks were.

The alarm went off at exactly 2:00 and we all slipped silently out of our sleeping bags. Carrot, Dan's brother and Ted started a small fire while Dan and I got into the brakeless truck. The night was as black as coal with a scent of wet grass and the cold sting of mountain air.

Dan pulled a rifle from the back of the truck and I almost fainted when I saw it: an old Winchester .22-short, single-shot, roughly equivalent to a sling shot.

I looked at the spotlight mounted on the truck and Dan read my mind. "The wiring is a little off, I know, but it usually works after I flip the switch on and off, and then back on again, so don't worry," he said.

"OK," I said. "Give me the gun."

We drove to the crest of the hill as quietly as possible. Dan kept the Plymouth in first and almost idled it into position. I shoved a shell into the breech of the rifle and winced; it seemed like putting a peanut inside a bean shooter. When we reached our launching point, Dan rotated the truck like a military tank and started revving the engine. The sound began as a low growl that grew in volume until a thousand screaming pieces of metal and all six pistons seemed ready to explode. The engine's roar echoed from the mountains and along the valley floor as the truck rattled and trembled. Dan took the engine higher, then even higher until I thought I could hear pieces of the truck's frame falling off. Just when I thought the vehicle would blow up and take us with it, Dan let her rip, popping the clutch and pushing the accelerator to the floor.

The pastoral elegance and evening serenity of the Hum Bug Valley were suddenly shattered by the Plymouth's glaring headlights. The valley floor was coming at us very fast and I could see silver frost shining on the meadow grass and the eyes of fifty or sixty deer turning curiously toward the apparition now screaming toward them at fifty miles an hour. Their ears stood out like sails and some began to snort; a few others flagged their tails.

I glanced at the speedometer as I took the rifle off safety. The thin red needle went past sixty, reached sixty-five, then climbed almost to seventy as we bounced off a logging road and hit the slippery grass of the meadow. Dan aimed the truck at a trio of deer standing just to our left. The deer stared back in disbelief.

At forty feet it was obvious we were not going to hit any of them. At thirty I yelled for the spotlight and Dan responded quickly, swiveling it around and pointing it at five more deer that seemed frozen in the sudden light.

The first round went off and I knew I'd missed because the velocity of a Winchester .22 short is not much more than 500 feet a second, and I could see the tiny bullet arcing through the light like a tracer. It disappeared in the darkness and suddenly the entire herd of deer panicked and began running, hopping up and down and flying through the air. It looked like a National Geographic TV special—the one where peacefully grazing impala are suddenly charged by three prides of starving lions.

A light went on in one of the tents in the campground, followed quickly by a second and a third. The truck spun to a stop in the center of the meadow, only a few feet from Seedling Creek. Smoke poured from under the hood. Deer were everywhere, bounding in all directions. I loaded and reloaded as quickly as I could and continued firing at them.

"Cool it," Dan whispered as more lights went on in the tents and campers started pouring outside to look in our direction. "Cool it, man; maybe they won't see us."

Some guy dressed in red shorts raised a lantern, trying to see what in hell was going on out there in the meadow. "Goddammit," Dan said, "I can't get the frigging spotlight off, or the headlights either. Sonofabitch. The electrical circuit is shorted." He jerked his head toward the campers. "What are they doing?" he asked. "What in the hell are they doing? Do they see us?"

I saw a small boy join his father, holding his father's hand in front of their tent. They both stared at us and the poor kid was freaking out. Other campers came out of their tents and switched on lanterns. Dan and I were surrounded by a ring of lights.

The small boy pointed at us. "Look! They're shooting Bambi!" he screamed. "They're shooting Bambi! Mommy! Hurry! Hurry!" Mommy appeared and joined her husband. She had one of those miner's lights on her head. "Oh my God," she said. "Oh, dear God."

"That's it," Dan said. "We're out of here." I could hear the gears grinding as he shoved it in first, but we went nowhere. We were spinning out.

"Damn tires," Dan cursed. "Why can't capitalist societies make tires that last?"

Finally the balding Sears treads grabbed hold and we went bouncing into the darkness, with lights blazing in every tent behind us.

"It's time for Plan B," Dan said as we reached the dark sanctuary of the logging road. "I know what to do. It will be dawn in a little while. Reach into the glove box and get my knife." I did as he asked and found the knife, an old Army issue. I handed it to Dan, who took it without saying anything more.

We took a long, circuitous route back to our camp, where we found Carrot, Ted and Dan's brother huddled around the failing embers of the fire. Carrot was wearing a mask. "They won't be able to testify it was me," he muttered.

Nobody else said anything. They all just stared at Dan and me as the last lights finally went out in the neighboring tents.

Dan reached into the fire pit, extracted several pieces of charcoal and began rubbing them on his face. Next he asked to borrow Ted's black wool stocking cap and put it on. Then, clenching the army knife in his teeth, he dropped to hands and knees and began crawling slowly into the meadow, heading toward the four or five deer remaining after our earlier assault. The rest of us stood and watched, shivering in the cold air.

The meadow grass wasn't that high and we could see Dan easily. So could the deer. But Dan seemed to know what he was doing, because he'd crawl forward only when the blacktail dropped their heads to feed.

It must have taken thirty minutes for him to get as close as he ever did, which was about a hundred feet from the nearest doe. We watched incredulously as he jumped to his feat and rushed toward the deer, waving the army knife in his hand. The deer came to attention and bounded away easily.

By then it was almost light and the first camper was going down to Seedling Creek to get water for cooking and cleaning. She looked up and saw Dan with his black face and black woolen cap, dropped her water and started screaming for some guy named Henry. Shouts of "Henrreeeeeeee!" echoed across Hum Bug Valley until all the campers were up again and wandering around in their pajamas. It was awful.

Now what? I wondered.

Carrot said maybe we should leave early to go gooseberry digging. The others agreed, but I told them I couldn't go. The marijuana seedlings had to be transplanted today or I would lose them. So they went off without me.

I spent the morning busily transplanting the seedlings into the 200 egg cartons Thelma had given me. I was just finishing up when a green pickup truck bearing a U.S. Forest Service emblem pulled up at our camp. A man wearing a ranger's uniform got out and I was glad to see he wasn't wearing a gun. He looked curiously at all the picnic tables I had arranged in a row one table wide and almost fifty feet long. The tables were covered with neatly arranged egg cartons, each pocket filled with dark, rich earth barely concealing a marijuana seedling. I thought I could already hear them growing.

I also imagined the clang of a cell door and the look on my mother's face as they slammed it shut for thirty years. My throat was as dry as cotton and my knees trembled as the ranger walked over to me.

"Howdy, son," he said. "Do you have a moment? We need to talk about a few things. By the way, what do you have in the egg crates, and where are your friends . . . huh?" He leaned forward with his head tilted. Not a good sign.

I can either do this, or I can't, I thought to myself. Then I looked him in the eye and said: "My friends are off working, and these"—I pointed to the egg cartons—"are worms."

"Worms? What do you mean?"

"Well, I'm here to do a little fishing, you know, trout and all that, and I keep my worms in the cartons."

He glanced at Seedling Creek, then back at me, nodded as if what I'd said made sense, and sat down on a picnic table bench. His right elbow was inches away from a dozen plants that could have wrecked the rest of my life, and I could almost see electrical energy crackling out of the dirt. But the ranger couldn't, and apparently he had other things on his mind—such as Ted's performance in the pool and last night's affair.

I apologized for Ted and promised to talk to him and make sure he'd never do such a thing again.

"What else are you doing here?" the ranger asked. I told him about our groovy relationship with the Forest Service and how I wanted to be a ranger when I got out of school—in fact, how most of us wanted to be rangers, even Carrot—and that we did blister rust control work every summer for the district office in Susanville. I looked humbly at the ground and kicked a little dirt with the toe of my boot. "Know any of those boys up there?" I asked in my best forest ranger voice.

He cleared his throat and said he didn't, but someone had reported people shooting at deer in the meadow last night, and did I know anything about that? I'm sure he knew I was lying when I said I didn't, but for reasons beyond me he didn't pursue the matter. He just looked around our camp and said in a nice tone of voice that there was a limit on the time you could stay in a federal campground and it would probably be best if we picked up our things and moved along so someone else could have a turn at the campsite.

I almost knocked him over as I began picking up things and packing them away, meanwhile glancing furtively at the egg cartons. What if one of the damn things sprouted while he was still there?

But he got back in his truck and I waved as he drove away, then began straightening the wood pile and sweeping the grounds while he watched in his rear-view mirror.

When Dan, Carrot, Ted and Dan's brother returned that afternoon I had most of the camp cleaned up—my stuff, anyway—and when I told Carrot what had happened I thought he would faint away.

Dan wanted to stay despite the ranger's advice, arguing that nobody could prove anything. But I knew better and reluctantly began pouring the contents of the egg cartons into Seedling Creek. The seedlings were caught up in swirls of cold creek water and floated away, gone forever.

The whole damn thing made me think again about what Ted had done. Who could possibly do such a thing in a trout stream? Maybe Ted's shenanigan had loosened the entire ball of karmic string, but that still didn't explain the ranger's clemency. He had us dead to rights. I watched and wondered as more earthy clots of Panama Red fell from the cardboard cartons.

Maybe some of the sprouts would lodge in a muddy wedge of riverbank and take root. Perhaps someday I'd return and find out. By then I'd also surely be an expert with a dead-drifted nymph.

But for now, this was the end; it was time to leave or go to jail. Ted sealed the deal by reminding us we were almost out of smokes and down to our last six-pack. "Six Olys and one lid left," he said. "Let's do the lid, brothers, as we get the hell out of here."

The road out passed other campsites but for some reason no one watched us go. The flaps were down on all the tents as we drove by, though there may have been a shotgun or two poking out a window; we didn't pause to look. Instead, we motored on with a billowing cloud of Panama Red (always our favorite) pouring out the truck windows and drifting through the limbs of the forests we had undoubtedly saved.

I thought Dan was shifting a little on the late side and he missed third a couple of times, but he was in the middle of a very serious dissertation on the Beatles while we passed the joint back and forth. He was doing fifty and looking over at me, delivering his final argument, when I saw the timbered bridge coming up. I knew it was too late and he'd never make the downshift; we wouldn't have made it even if we'd had brakes.

Somehow, part of the truck caught on one of the bridge timbers and kept us from flying all the way over the edge and straight down 200 feet. The truck came to a stop hanging almost vertically over the side of the bridge.

I found myself pressed up against the dashboard, looking down at the rusting remains of another vehicle that hadn't made it across the bridge. The bridge shuddered and the truck lurched several inches more, threatening to continue falling and kill us all. Then suddenly it was quiet.

For a moment the silence was complete. Then I began to hear faint noises from the back of the truck. Dan's brother, Carrot, and Ted each crawled slowly and carefully along the side of the pickup, then over the timber to safety. From the corner of my eye I could see Dan with me in the front seat, pale as a summer cloud and trembling—the only time I ever saw him afraid. As for me, I was afraid to move.

But staying put wasn't an alternative. I like to think I have a delicate touch, but I've never put my hands on anything with the same sensitivity as I did when I reached for the door handle. It took about three minutes to get the door open and I expected the timber to give way and the truck to start slipping any moment. But the truck never moved.

Once outside I had to crawl along the edge of the truck bed, never breathing until I finally reached the edge of the bridge and safety.

Carrot was standing in the center of the bridge, peeing. Ted was lying flat on his back, picking up dirt clods and dropping them again and saying "Eeny, meeny, miney mo." Dan's brother was walking around in circles.

Dan also got out safely too and offered everyone another Red, remarking how cool it was that we had all survived and apologizing for his driving error. Everyone looked at him oddly, like dogs look at each other after a fight when it's obvious the loser isn't the leader anymore.

Dan's brother walked up to him, looked him in the eye and said: "Man, you're a piece of shit." Carrot nodded in agreement. Even Ted didn't argue.

Dan made a valiant effort to reclaim the leader's role. "If you guys don't come back and help me get my truck off this bridge you get none of the money from our last two lots," he threatened. "I'm keeping it all."

But it was too late. We turned away from him and started walking toward the highway, some ten miles away.

It was dark by the time we reached Interstate 36 and we had to split up to try to hitch rides. I paired with Ted and Carrot paired with Dan's brother, leaving Dan to hitch alone. Of course he got a ride right away. Then somebody picked up Carrot and Dan's brother.

But the cars kept speeding past Ted and me, and the people inside them looked at us strangely. I could understand that; it was because Ted's hair was so crazy. His Afro hadn't been trimmed in a year and was full of burrs. He was also wearing an Elmer Fudd necklace, which probably didn't help.

While we waited I told Ted that I'd thought we were all dead when the truck went off the bridge, and before that I'd thought I was about to get caught with the illegal plants and spend the rest of my life in jail.

"Well, you could have," he said, "but you didn't. We're OK. Anyway, I'd have come to see you at least once a month. Here, have a toke. What about Diane? What are you going to do when you get back and we graduate?"

"I don't know," I told him. "I love her, but I think she's gone. Have you seen the way she still looks at Tim Worthington? What in hell does she see in him? How can she still love that guy after the way he's treated her? I don't know what's going to happen. I wonder what will happen to all of us. Things are weird, aren't they?"

"Yeah they are, and people are crazy. Most of them, anyway. They look at something and can't see it, or else they look and see something that isn't even there. That's why they don't like jazz and their politics are all screwed up."

He continued. "Me, I've joined the Peace and Freedom Party and I've decided to go to graduate school and get my credential. I'd like to teach someday. I don't know about the other guys. Maybe they'll just get old and fat and live in the suburbs until they die."

"Maybe," I agreed, sticking out my thumb for the next car. "But I'll never be like that. I'll never change. I just know it."

A car stopped and we got a ride.

I saw Dan a few times on campus after that, although we never said much to one another and I don't know whatever became of him. I heard that he went back and pulled his truck off the bridge, but I don't know if that was true or not. His brother went on to an acting career, but I finally lost track of him, too.

Ted became an English teacher and after we graduated we hitchhiked together through South America and Europe. But that's another story, and now it has been thirty years since I've seen him.

Carrot was drafted right after the trip to Seedling Creek and never made it back. He was killed during the Tet Offensive in Vietnam.

Diane and I went out a few more times and I guess I was still in love with her for a while, but somehow I'd learned enough to know when it was time to let things go. The time came when I got a phone call from a well endowed co-ed who liked to breathe from aerosol cans on dates. She was headed for the Peace Corps in Bolivia and wanted to see me just one more time before she left.

Which I did, cans and all, although I never went back to see if any of my plants had taken root along the shores of Seedling Creek. I'm sure however, that the big brown I lost is still there. Those things seem to live forever.

River of Giants

Back in 1972 my adolescent hero, fly-fishing legend Joe Brooks, published a book called *Trout Fishing*. It took me by storm, best evidenced by the confession that, more than once, I slept with it under my pillow and, in fact, dreamed about it constantly—especially the color photo at the top of page 287.

It was a picture of a giant steelhead, the most beautiful fish I had ever seen. The skin on its back was steel blue, exactly the color of river fog on a cold morning. A slash of Chinese red—the color of bright blood—ran down its flanks, and its cartilage and muscle glowed with the shades of an October sunrise. The fish weighed more than twenty pounds, the book said, and from that point there would be no difference between the steelhead on page 287 and everything I had ever wanted from a trout.

"I am convinced that one steelhead I lost in the Babine in early October of 1970 was an all-time record," Brooks wrote. "I knew from the moment he hit me I would never stop him. But I tried. I followed him quite a way downstream but suddenly felt a slack line. When I reached the spot where the end of the fly line lay on the water I found that he had merely dropped the fly. That fish had to be at least forty pounds." Those words changed my life. Forever.

Brooks was not the only one to write about the Babine River. John Fennelly, in a small but important little book called *Steelhead Paradise* said some interesting (but not always quite accurate) things about the river. Bob Nauheim, a well-known West Coast angler who one day would become my friend, later wrote an article about the Babine for *Outdoor Life* magazine. His title, "The River of Giants," seemed absolutely perfect; it not only defined the run of fish that ascended the river each fall but also described many of the fishermen who cast their lines into the Babine's beautifully dark, tea-colored water. Bob's story set the hook deeper in me. I wanted to go.

Then Dave Whitlock, another writer who would eventually cross my path and leave his mark on me as both fisherman and friend, published a story about the Babine. "The steelhead of the Babine are second to none in size and power," he said, and when I read those words I knew it was time to head north. Dave's story included the name and telephone number of a lodge where he had fished. I dialed the number and asked if I could come up with a few friends, see the river and fish at the camp.

It was October 12, 1978, when I reached the Babine. A cold morning mist hovered over the river and several brightly painted wooden skiffs lay anchored next to the half-frozen shoreline. Red and yellow cottonwood and aspen leaves shook and rattled in the wind and although I could not see them, I knew beyond doubt that somewhere in the river was the fish of my lifetime.

The Wickwire family was there to greet me—Bob; his wife, Jerrie Lou; their son, Jud, and daughter, Cynthia. They stood in front of a tiny cluster of hand-made cabins and a black chimney that sent spirals of blue smoke high into the Canadian sky.

I had many questions. About Joe Brooks and all the others who had been there before me, about all the pools, about the race of shadowy ancient steelhead. Bob and Jerrie Lou tried to answer them as other anglers waited patiently around the dinner table that first night. As they spoke, I began to feel something I'd never felt before: This river wasn't just a place to fish; it was much more than that. It seemed to flow through the log-cabin windows and into my senses with a pounding roar and rich scent of salmon and dark brown earth. And, as strange as it might sound, it held a promise. "If you stay here," it seemed to say, "you will learn and see much, and a good part of your life will go as this river goes."

At the time I had no idea what this meant, and I went to bed uneasy, restless beneath a sky of blazing stars and the swirl of Arctic lights, drifting in and out of a dreamless sleep, with the sound of Arctic wolves all around me.

Next morning arrived soundless, cold and damp. The river was visible through my cabin window and I watched it for a long time. I could see the forest, wet from rain and bright with burning fall colors along the riverbanks. A large, smooth boulder creased the center of the pool where I would fish, forming a metaphorical question mark in the currents that curled around and around before disappearing in a push of foam that came from somewhere I couldn't see. Maybe a steelhead would be there, in the part of the question mark that turned into a straight line, a seam of water perfect for holding something I wanted more than anything else in the world.

On the far bank stood a lone cottonwood, one of the largest I had ever seen. Although it wasn't on the river's edge, it threw a long dagger of red, yellow and orange reflections across the surface. The river danced beneath the colors as if it knew they were there and enjoyed them.

"Fish that seam well," Bob Wickwire had said the night before. "There's almost always at least one big steelhead in front of that rock."

I remember looking at my skinny legs as I pulled on my waders. I was afraid and unsure of myself. Was I ready for the river of giants? Was I good enough? Would I succeed or fail? I'd caught steelhead on other rivers, but this river and its steelhead were different, and I knew it the moment I saw it. The Babine ran with electricity in its current, unchanged since the beginning of time and charged by the forces that hold everything in nature together. And at that moment,

I understood the reality of a river, and its unassailable position in the natural order, and its immunity from the political processes and definitions of those who walk its shore.

I realized no one ever owns a river like this. It cannot be bought or sold. We can only fish it or borrow it, use it or spend much of our lives on it, and in the process perhaps become something more than we once were.

Two mornings later I was still looking for my first fish. I was standing on the rocky beach of a stretch called the Home Run, rigging up, when young Cynthia Wickwire came up and asked if she could make a cast or two.

"No problem," I replied, certain she wouldn't even be able to flip over the bail of her spinning reel without help. She stood on a wet, slippery rock the size and color of a very large, overripe cantaloupe, with a bottle of Coke in one hand and a magazine tucked under her other arm. Suddenly she began swinging her spinning rod around and around, high over her head, faster and faster, until the four-inch lure on the end of the line traced a blazing circular orbit that looked exactly like a helicopter rotor whirling in the sky.

Then she launched the lure like a rocket. It went higher and higher over the Home Run until it finally plunked down right in front of a large boulder. The lure had barely touched the surface when she set the hook in a steelhead. Fifteen minutes later the exhausted steelhead came obediently to Cynthia's feet, like a trained seal.

She eyed the creature with a tilt of her head, then took a swig of Coke and jerked the lure out of the steelhead's mouth in a dazzling display of dental artistry I never expect to see again. The steelhead shook its head a few times, then turned and swam away, no doubt thoroughly confused by the sequence of events.

"My God," I said, "how much did that thing weigh?"

"Oh, I don't really know, about eighteen pounds, I guess," Cynthia said. "It was a female. You can tell by how silvery she was."

Without saying another word she made a second cast, this time sending the lure through the crisp morning air to the far side of the boulder from which she had just snatched the first unsuspecting fish. Her fluttering silver messenger dropped quietly and precisely into the slot next to the boulder. Even from seventy-five feet away I could see it wobbling and flashing in the current, a hypnotic metallic dance of light and seductive movement.

The lure hadn't traveled six feet when a large buck rolled up from the depths of the pool like a killer whale in a feeding frenzy. Once again Cynthia set the hook with a powerful sweep of her arms and the second fish soon came ashore like the first. It looked as large as a horse to a fly fisherman who had never seen a steelhead much over ten pounds.

Cynthia read my mind. "About twenty-one pounds, but probably not much more," she said. "This one is a buck, you know." She released the trophy just as she had the first.

"How old are you?" I asked.

"I'm ten years old," she said. "Here, you want to try a cast?"

"No, uh...no, thanks, that's all right."

"Well, OK, but I have to go now, anyway. I'm supposed to be helping Mom bake an apple pie."

She turned like a hummingbird and glided away over the rocky shore, carrying her fishing rod, her now-empty Coke bottle and her magazine under one wing, then disappeared into the lodgepole cabin and closed the door.

I turned back to the pool, lifted my rod and rolled over the heavy fly line in an enthusiastic roll cast that went nowhere in particular, drawing the fly to the surface in a determined effort to take a third steelhead, probably a new world record, from that very rock where Cynthia had found the first two.

It was one of a thousand casts I would make that week. I fished hard on every pool. I fell in the river at least three times, left countless flies hopelessly snagged on the rocks of most of the water I fished, and four days later, just after supper—and one of the best apple pies I ever tasted—right there on the Home Run, I finally hooked up just as the sun was setting.

"Fish on! Fish on!" I screamed as the entire population of the camp emptied from the cabins to witness the battle. I was an interesting proposition. The other anglers were cool hands indeed, experienced and intense. Everyone knew that I was, to that point, without a catch and their concern only amplified mine.

The line hissed darkly in the river and for ten minutes the powerful fish held steady, swimming and scraping around ragged boulders and ledgerock. Then, after a series of thrashing explosions in the water, it finally came toward the beach, pushing a wall of water ahead of it.

I stared out into the growing darkness for a glimpse of the steelhead. The moment of truth was approaching, when the tangled, worn leader would either hold or break. The wind stirred high in the trees and the first star appeared in the chill evening. I heard a voice and knew Cynthia was there, for it was her melody floating in the air.

"How big is it?" she asked.

"I don't know," someone else replied.

"What? What in the hell is it? Is it a buck or a hen?"

"I can't see it yet. Get a flashlight or something."

A yellow beam cut instantly through the darkness, a long shaft of light going farther and farther into the black water until it came to rest in a muddy soup of cold gravel and the spiraling thrash of a silver fish. She weighed a solid fifteen pounds, heavy and strong with red gills, deep flanks and a belly of pearl. I could not have been prouder. The water fell from her tail in a sweet rain, luminescent in the cold night, impossible to forget, or to lower. Twenty seven years later she is still there, breathing in front of me, her silhouette as clean as a razor.

Cynthia's brother, Jud, was two years older than his sister. He was already a river guide at age twelve and had been a member of the select Babine River Giant Steelhead club for eight seasons, having subdued a twenty-eight-pound steelhead when he was only four years old. Everyone said he was almost as good as his father with a rod and a boat. I don't know about that, and I try to stay out of family discussions of that type, but in the years to come I would learn just how good he really was. It became sort of a silent game for me to see if he would ever make a mistake with the boat and hit a rock—not those he bumped as he slid the boat ashore, for those never count, but those touched while he negotiated some of the trickiest, boulder-strewn water I have ever seen. After we fished together eighteen years, the number was exactly three.

The third member of the Wickwire clan, Jerrie Lou, was wearing an apron the day I met her and I soon concluded it had been sewn to her skin not long after she came into the world, for it was a long time before I ever saw her without it. She was a sorceress, a keeper of many secrets, one who could make delicious pastries, pies and some of the best soups on the planet from ingredients so simple it seemed impossible.

She also had a sense of humor. She searched the riverbank until she found a stone the exact size, shape and color of a pork sausage. Then, when she met someone she really liked, she would warm it up in her stove and put it on the person's breakfast plate next to the most perfectly prepared eggs you could imagine. She would even go so far as to coat the thing with cooking oil until it glistened with mouth-watering reality. I considered it a great compliment when I tried the sausage one morning and found it made of rock.

I watched Jerrie Lou for twenty years on the Babine, holding the fort, the family, the lodge and the clients together in an embrace of affection and concern so powerful that longtime river rats, politicians, first-time steelheaders, useless fish bums and expert anglers from all over the world, all of them, would come to fish at the lodge, fall in love with her and then do almost anything for a second helping of her famous desserts. But we loved her most of all for a smile that came from the sun itself, one that could melt the coldest heart and light up a day's fishing no matter how high, cold or dirty the water might be. If the Babine had a disposition too volatile to predict, then Jerrie Lou was made of patience all too rare in the world of fishing.

Bob Wickwire stood at the head of the family, and if you knew him then you knew where the buck stopped. I learned more about traditional steelheading from him than anyone else, the lessons coming slowly from watching and imitating him and listening to the things he said on a river he knew better than anyone.

He was there the day I hooked a memorable fish many miles down-river at a place no one had fished before, a place I came to call the Triple Header. Bob was seated on a rock, watching my line swing through the sweep of the best tailout I will ever see. Without warning, the shallow water suddenly blew apart with the rise of an immense steelhead. The rod bowed to the strain and the line went tight; I had him.

"Holy Cow!" Bob yelled, jumping to his feet and balancing impossibly on the top of the boulder. "That's two monsters you've hooked this trip."

He stayed with me as I followed the fish downriver. Nearly an hour passed before we could finally see the living shadow in the water. "Oh, man, I wish Jud could be here to see this," Bob whispered. He knelt and taped the steelhead for me, then raised the fish into the sunlight of a September afternoon. It was beautiful beyond anything I had ever seen.

"It's thirty pounds, maybe a little more," Bob said. "I get a measurement of forty-by-twenty-four."

I was exhausted, soaked with sweat and trembling. My fingers were cramped from the struggle and my breath came in quick gasps. "I've had enough, Bob," I said. "I can't fish any more. I have to quit."

He smiled. "Oh no you don't. Look what I see downriver." He pointed at the next pool.

"What do they call that?" I asked.

"It doesn't have a name," he replied. "You better go down there and catch another steelhead. Then you can name it whatever you want."

"Are you sure?"

"Yes."

"How does the water look? Is it any good?"

"It looks perfect. Really good."

We left immediately.

By then we had been fishing together five years, and we did the same for another fifteen. Bob always maintained a loyal following of anglers who came to the Babine to learn from him and share the sport of steelheading. We didn't always see eye to eye, but I knew the real deal when I saw it. It's easy to be sentimental about such matters, but if you watch twenty seasons of a man's life pass by on a river he loves and helped to define, you'll see things you can never forget. And I haven't. Bob and his family were in fact pioneers of the Babine. Their legacy remains.

The Babine also hosted another family who would leave their mark on all who came there. Joy and Ejnar Madsen were married in 1956 and by 1957 their lodge, "Norlakes," had evolved into a family owned and operated business. Like Bob and Jerrie Lou Wickwire, Joy and Ejnar had a dream of creating an internationally famous fishing lodge. And they succeeded. I remember seeing Ejnar going by in the early morning mist like a ghostly sentimental. No one gripped the steering arm of an outboard like he did. Sometimes I would wave, if I thought he could see me, and if he did he would raise his arm in a salute and then disappear in the metallic roar and cold morning fog. Now and then, if Bob wasn't looking he'd come over and we would talk steelheading, but the moments were carefully guarded. Bob and Ejnar respected one another but they were also fierce competitors. I stayed out of their way and admired both simultaneously.

Joy was the official greeting committee for Norlakes and I would see her in the Smithers airport each fall season. She loved her work and, from what I could tell, she usually had the toughest guests and all their luggage under her arm and spell in about five minutes. Her dignity and polite charm were unsurpassed and as one angler said, "Joy could tell someone to go to hell and they'd look forward to the trip." Ejnar passed away in 1983 and Joy now lives in the wine country of Northern California. Now and then, when I think about it, or look at some of the old photographs I can see the thread that Joy and Ejnar wove through the water and stones of the Babine. The mark is still there.

~

Certain questions inevitably arise whenever Babine steelhead are discussed: How do they get so big? Why does it happen? What size can they really attain? As far as I know, nobody has ever answered these questions definitively. Some people say the typically long freshwater residency of juvenile steelhead in the Babine creates a larger smolt, one able to capitalize immediately on larger food items once it reaches salt water, giving it a head start on growth. Others claim a similarly long salt-water residency makes the fish larger. Both answers seem obvious, but they fail to address the question of why these steelhead should have such a life cycle. The answer probably lies in genetics, but whatever genetic secret the Babine steelhead possess apparently is not transferable. To my knowledge, every attempt to transplant Babine steelhead to other rivers has resulted in returns of only average-sized fish, identical in proportion to the river's original inhabitants.

"It's the size of those rocks and boulders," one angler once told me as we watched a forty-two-inch buck emerge from two feet of water with a 1/0 Green Butt Skunk in the corner of its huge jaw. "They're simply too big for a small fish to move around for a (spawning) redd. The little fish just can't do it."

I considered this remark while watching long columns of pink salmon and sockeye go by in the Babine, hour after hour, day after day, throughout all of September and sometimes, well into October. Some of these salmon weighed barely four pounds. If they are successful in spawning, and I believe they are, then one would have to assume that all sizes of steelhead could do the same and there should be more small steelhead in the river.

But whatever the reason, Bob Nauheim was right: the Babine is indeed a river of giants. The length and girth measurements of its fish provide ample evidence. Most experienced anglers assume the girth of a steelhead will be approximately half its length, especially on females. It can, of course, be larger or smaller, but the one-half ratio seems a good rule of thumb.

The largest female I've ever heard of stretched the tape to a nifty forty inches with a girth just at twenty inches. I've seen countless females in the thirty-six- to thirty-nine-inch class and in almost every one the girth was very close to half the length. By late October, after the fish have been in the river for some time, some tend to have smaller girths, as you would expect. For obvious reasons, the males seem to lose more girth than the females.

I've heard reliable reports of two forty-five-inch Babine steelhead, both males; unfortunately, no girth measurements were taken of these two so we can only guess their weight. I've seen so many bucks in the thirty-nine- to forty-two-inch range that I've lost count. Girths on such fish usually run from nineteen to twenty-three or twenty-four inches, but can go much higher.

Skeena Indian groups claim to have taken fifty-pound steelhead in nets, and I understand it is theoretically possible for a steelhead to grow that large if it survives multiple spawning and ocean migrations.

A photo taken in the early 1990s shows a woman angler holding what she believed was a large king salmon, one approaching forty-five pounds. The fish was cleaned and eaten before anyone thought to look twice at the photo. It was a male steelhead, taken on a lure from the main Skeena River.

In August, 1998, Mike O'Neill, then president of the B.C. Wildlife Federation's Northwest Region, sent me a facsimile describing two Skeena steelhead captured in a test net at the Tyee counting station. They weighed forty-two and forty-one pounds respectively a day after they were captured. The measurements were forty-two-by-twenty-six and a half inches and forty-one and a half-by-twenty-six inches.

~

The Wickwire and Madsen families were absolutely critical to the preservation of the Babine River steelhead. Bob and Jud Wickwire for example, provided estimates of annual escapement and spawning populations in the river, and spent countless hours watching, floating and fishing over schools of great fish and reporting their findings to local fisheries biologists.

The river was fished hard during the late 1950s and into the mid-1960s by anglers using hardware and bait. Many were legitimate experts at these types of fishing; others were little more than greedy fishermen who came just to kill their limit of wild steelhead averaging an incredible fifteen pounds. As far as they were concerned, as long as they got their limit everything else could go to hell—and it probably would have were it not for the Wickwires and Joy and Ejnar Madsen and a few fisheries biologists, including Bob Hooten.

Bob Wickwire remembers days when sixty fish or more were hooked in a single outing by an angler and guide trolling Hot Shots or other lures. Nearly one in six of these fish weighed twenty pounds or more. Bob knew all too well what would happen if the slaughter was allowed to continue. At his suggestion, and after several seasons of hard work and gritty political lobbying by those who felt as he did, catch limits finally were reduced—and with them the numbers of fishermen who measured success by steelhead body counts.

All along, of course, only the largest steelhead were taken, slaughtered as trophies, then transported back to camp sometimes floating like ghosts in the tepid bilge of a warm transom. I remember one cold, drizzly October day when three fishermen pulled their boat ashore and asked if I thought their dead fish would weigh twenty pounds.

"We want this one for the wall," one said. "Charlie here caught it just a few moments ago. Ain't it a honey?"

I looked away for a moment, for I couldn't bear the sight of a once-perfect steelhead that may have weighed twenty pounds—nor could I stand to see the brutal marks left by several blows to its head and shoulders from the steel hammer lying in the boat. I hoped the rain would get worse and maybe the three anglers would give up and go home if they thought Charlie had his trophy. "Twenty pounds?" I said. "You bet it will. Maybe more."

In 1981 the limit was reduced to one fish a day, then a little later a zero-kill rule was initiated. The frozen meat-locker gang grumbled and complained, but most eventually disappeared—especially after the license fees and cost of a week's fishing began to go up.

The higher costs excluded a good many decent sportsmen, too, and for that I can only express regret—though I had always secretly believed that fishing the trophy Canadian rivers during the 1970s and early '80s was inappropriately inexpensive. There are places in the angling world where bargain-basement mentalities and philosophies are acceptable, even necessary, but in my opinion, such concepts don't apply to the opportunity to entice a seagoing rainbow trout weighing more than twenty-five pounds from a river so wild and free you almost have to travel back in time just to reach it and make your cast.

With the no-kill rule, many of the essentials for preservation were in place. Everyone knew there would be no steelhead hatcheries on the Babine. Neither would there be any more bait sacks filled with steelhead roe, nor any more trophies lying in their own milt, spawning even as they died. Anglers talked excitedly about the river's future.

Then Bob and Jerrie Lou Wickwire received government approval for a new guiding license. They telephoned and I listened with growing interest as they described plans to build a new camp downriver. I was invited to participate and take over the reservations and bookings, and in the fall of 1983 we opened the doors of a place called Silver Hilton.

And as it turned out, my early predictions were true. It became personal. And professional. The river entered the stream of my life and I have returned each season now for more than twenty five years. I could easily do another twenty-five. The Wickwire family sold Silver Hilton to Stephen Myers in 1998. Steve's commitment to the river is unsurpassed and he has improved upon the traditions established long ago as he and long time Babine friend and angler John Ferguson along with others, continue fighting to protect the river and its remarkable steelhead. The two upriver camps are still in operation; Pierce and Anita Clegg purchased the upper lodge from Ejnar and Joy Madsen sometime in the early 1980's and have added much to the history of the Babine. Chick Stewart purchased Bob Wickwires old camp about the same time and remains active.

Most recently, the three lodges have formed The Babine River Foundation and the struggle to preserve the river continues against odds which at times seem formidable indeed. This struggle has become no small part of my life as an angler and citizen, and I have known for some time now, that if one is to praise a river publicly, as I have this one for so many years, and enjoy the circumstances it offers, as I have for all these years, then sooner or later one must engage those things which could destroy it.

Current issues faced by The Babine River Foundation include the integration of appropriate and environmentally sustainable logging, angling management plans which will prevent overcrowding and loss of the wilderness character of the watershed, and modification of commercial netting philosophies and techniques, from "mixed stock fishing," to a truly selective harvest, so that the interception of wild Babine steelhead in nets is reduced to a minimum.

As these new issues have emerged, the flame has passed from one generation to another, and today the River of Giants lies in the glove of good hands—those for whom the words "impossible odds" have no meaning.

"Next Time"

I have always loved fine tackle. This reel was no exception. It was made at a time when ornate embellishment and serious devotion to craftsmanship were considered inseparable and essential for a good product.

Even the factory box was decorated with a careful hand, the design, trademark and logo done in elegant cursive. The reel itself was stout and heavy, solid brass and hardened steel, polished and ready to go, with finely tooled symmetrical engravings so delicate they looked like steel lace. On the left side plate was an agate bearing, set like a jewel in a knurled button for drag adjustment. On top was a level-wind gate that paced back and forth when the spool was turned so that the line always stayed in place, stored in perfect order, always ready for the next cast. The dual black-and-silver handles curled so gracefully they appeared to be in motion even when they were not.

The reel was labeled "Pflueger Summit" and it had been manufactured somewhere around 1948. For years it rested inside my father's tackle box just beneath the steel trays holding hand-carved Heddon bait-casting plugs with names like "River Runt," "Crippled Minnow," "Crazy Crawler," "Ding Bat" and "Spook," right next to the magical assemblage of other things needed for fishing. But I liked the reel best.

Sometimes, during the winter, my father would take it out and polish it, then turn the handle and watch as the gate moved back and forth, laying down line from a remembered catch. Deep inside the gears of that reel were the marks of wear from a thousand black bass and northern pike, a musky or two, and pan fish beyond counting.

I knew this because he said so and I believed him, even though things weren't always easy between us. Almost from the beginning there were unresolved differences, an invisible netting of quiet anger, and finally arguments that seemed impossible to mend. Nevertheless, we fished together, first for bass when I was still a boy, trolling up and down a lake cloaked in the scents of dry pine, yellow grass and early morning fog and saturated with the sweet feel of a wet bass going from hand to stringer at dawn.

But there was more to it than just fishing. It also was a way for the two of us to be together away from normal responsibilities and disagreements. I hoped the endeavor might also help me find a way to be closer to him.

We also hunted, and he taught me how to shoot and be safe with guns. As a teenager I hunted with him for blacktail in California and mule deer in Western Nevada, but after shooting exactly two I lost interest and turned full time to rivers. Eventually my father gave up hunting, too, and for the same reasons—neither of us liked the killing. He turned to steelhead and salmon fishing instead, then later to the pursuit of brook, rainbow and brown trout in Montana. We fished together for steelhead and salmon in the rivers of northern California; by then I was a young man and things finally were beginning to be different between us. I was outgrowing my youth and at the same time I could see the envelope of old age gathering around him, clouding his eyes and taking the strength from his arms.

I began to worry—about him, about us. He was wracked by emphysema and it was killing him a day at a time, spreading over him like a dark shadow until he began to look small and weak, with brown spots on his skin and in his lungs. But I still enjoyed listening to his stories, and sometimes now even told a few myself, and in the process we both found something more than either of us had bargained for: We talked about fishing not just because we loved it, but because we had discovered at last that we also loved each other—even though, oddly enough, we never said so. I always regretted that.

He bore his illness with determination, fierce stubbornness and courage, but in the last few months the life was draining out of him hour by hour and he knew it. The worry I felt for him was a new experience, as was the need to help care for him when I visited. I found myself wishing we were out fishing for steelhead or salmon, and I wanted to turn back the hands of the clock and somehow get him out of the mess he was in.

At night my dreams sometimes brought the image of a pale, thin, detached hand, reaching toward me out of the darkness. Only the hand could be seen, as if illuminated by a spot light and in the light I could see distorted veins, the soft skin of old age, and long, skeletal fingers with ragged nails. I would reach out to take the grotesque hand—really more of a claw—and grasp it firmly, knowing it was his, and I would try to tell him I loved him and that somehow everything would be all right.

Sometimes I'd reach past the floating hand and try to find the rest of him, but I never could, at least not in the way I wanted to. Instead, I'd wake up, go into the kitchen, and make him some toast with strawberry jelly. He would smile, and while I tried to repress the thought of a skeletal hand without an arm attached, I'd put my own arms around him. But I never said much when I did it and the moment always passed, unspoken into oblivion.

Then one day, during a summer visit, he gave me the Pflueger reel. I hadn't thought about the reel for years, but when I accepted the gift I knew exactly what it meant.

Our last fishing trip began at dawn on a cold winter day that next autumn. The river was too high and fast for him to wade; so I carried him on my back, across the river to an island where we hoped to fish for fresh-run steelhead. When we reached the island we found another fisherman in the spot I had wanted to fish; he already had a solitary fish lying face down in the cold dirt. It was a large brown trout, almost six pounds, unusual for most Pacific Northwest steelhead rivers but fairly common among some of the Central Valley rivers of Northern California.

The angler, if such a term can be justified, had just unhooked the fish and resumed fishing, leaving the dying brown trout stranded on the shore, its gills working frantically and its eyes bulging. My father looked down at the dying fish and watched its futile attempts to breathe. Sand and mud obscured the brightness of the trout, and its red spots and amber halos. It lay there helplessly, drowning in the air, sightless and desperate.

I remember the look in my father's eyes as he gripped his portable oxygen bottle and watched the trout die. I wasn't certain what to do, so I simply leaned over and hoisted him up on my back and shoulders once more and started wading across the stream toward his truck.

As I stepped into the smooth current and looked down into the water where I would make my first step, I could see the reflection of clouds going by. Those reflections are something I never tire of seeing, but this morning they were different; it almost seemed as if the reflections remained at my feet while the clouds themselves continued on their way, crossing over the river and disappearing beyond the distant hills, until all the boundaries between earth, water and sky disappeared and there were no longer any differences in anything. Men die like trout, I thought, in the same muddy places and in the same dream, their life going out of them a breath at a time along with the best they ever were or could be, leaving only memories in the minds and hearts of those who had the good fortune of knowing them.

I listened to the river and the sounds of my father's labored breathing, and tried to keep my feet steady so I would not fall with him. When we were halfway across, with the roar of the river all around us, my father finally surrendered and broke down. I could feel the sudden trembling of his arms and legs, wrapped around me like those of a small child, as he began quietly to cry.

We made it safely to the other side just as the sun came up, orange and full of fire. I released him and we sat together in his truck, saying nothing as I searched for the words I needed. I knew this would be our last river together and I wanted to thank him for everything and confess my feelings for him, straightforwardly and without reservation, but the words just wouldn't come. In desperation I thought that if I looked around I might see something that would inspire such a conversation; so I studied the windshield of his truck, then the trees in the surrounding woods, but there was nothing—no sign, no symbol, not a single thing to help me say the things I wanted and needed to say.

How could this be? How could my father, who had always been as strong as steel, allow such a thing to happen to him? The thought came and went quickly as the wind stirred outside, coming from the north, cold and moist, carrying the scent of earth and moss, howling around the truck. I looked at him, sitting quietly on the front seat, dying in the silence, one breath at a time, next in line behind the trout we had left on the island.

I considered turning on the radio, but there was no music I wanted to hear. Then I thought of the first tiny fish my father had helped me catch so many years ago, floating in the air above the truck and watching us with the eyes of one who knew it all. Suddenly I wanted everything back, and even reached out for the fish, but it simply curled its tail and disappeared into the woods and the awkward silence.

"Listen," I said finally. "Did I ever tell you about the time I took Barbara Jenkins trout fishing?

"No, Son, you didn't. How was it?"

"It was great, Dad, just great. She couldn't cast ten feet, but she wore a bikini the entire time. You should have seen her in the water."

I looked into his eyes twice—once in the rear-view mirror that was turned sideways, just to make sure everything was OK and it was all right to continue, then directly at him.

He was smiling. "What in the hell happened?" he asked.

"Well, she finally hooked a small trout behind some rock in the middle of the stream; when she swung it up in the air and toward her, it fell off the hook and went down the top of her bathing suit. She started screaming so I had to reach in and land it for her."

He laughed, "Good God, you don't expect me to believe that, do you"?

"Yes, I do, because that's exactly the way it happened. More or less."

"Well, which was it? More? Or less?"

"I'm not sure," I answered.

On the evening he died my brother and I were with him and he was different; he was calm and easy. His hospital room was dim, with only a small lamp in the corner for light; he looked tired, thin and transparent, almost as if made of tissue. His hair had faded from black to almost snow white, but his eyes were still bright and blue.

We sat there talking about the way he felt. At one point I went outside to talk to his nurse; she said nothing more could be done and no one knew what to expect. She promised to call later that night if things got really bad. I knew what that meant, and swallowed once or twice before I went back into the room where my father would die, choosing my words carefully in the way you do when you know the hour is getting late. I don't remember what I said and it doesn't matter now.

As I watched the time running out of the eyes that could once see right through me, I saw the secret veil of my father recede as he began to speak. "Next time, I'll try to be more sensitive," he said with a knowing smile that cut me like a knife. He had never talked that way before. Not to anyone.

Then he closed his eyes for the last time and went to sleep. For a moment my brother and I watched him, thinking his words referred to our next visit in the hospital, then realizing there would be no more visits and he had known it before the words ever left his mouth.

I've often thought about those last words and what they might mean; they come to me whenever I think of him, or the hardships of his life, and how he changed when he became older. They come to me also in the things I learned from him and some that I discovered on my own; I see them also in the eyes of friends or strangers, those curious mirrors of life and windows to the soul where I see my own reflection, my own future.

Perhaps my father was right. Maybe there will be a next time for everybody, and a time after that, and even a time after that in a never-ending circle of rivers and life. If so, that's not so bad, and I would think that, maybe, if we do it enough times, somewhere along the way we'll get it right, and when the line goes out for the last time, we'll find something that really matters.

So, Dad, I'm almost sixty years old and I don't quite know how to finish this, but I wish I could have said it sooner: I love you. I always loved you.

And I still have the Pflueger.

"Ironwood Baby!"

Dick Larsen and I have drawn the lucky straw. We will, if necessary, crawl on bleeding hands and knees for as long as it takes to reach the heartland of this New Zealand wilderness river—this high-class, drop-your-waders-and-fork-over-the-bread, helicopter fly-out trophy trout river.

We know the stories: Alaskan resident trout shrink alongside those we will see today. Chile and Argentina will pale in the eye after this. God help us, even Montana waters will leave us yawning.

It looks good, the guides say. They always say that. It rained last night, and the temperature dropped a few degrees, perhaps enough to freshen the water and stir the salmon-sized brutes that lurk in the dark canyons and vertical ravines. We will see some suspended weightlessly in pools of clear water, looking like John McPhee's perfect metaphor: zeppelins. Others may be cruising and feeding in skinny tailouts, or hopefully at the head of runs, sifting mayfly nymphs and rummaging for anything they can find to eat. If we hit four cherries on the second pull of the casino trout-fishing machine, we might even find some taking cicadas from the surface like sharks feeding on bleeding meat.

I have fished the river before, but never the section we will fish today. If it runs true to form, there will be at least one monster in every pool, or maybe a pair, and sometimes, in the very largest pools, as many as a half dozen or more, browns and rainbows competing for space and food. Some of these will go off the end of the graph, exceeding even the limits of Larsen's imagination or my efforts to describe them.

"Geentlemen, you will see mòor trout theer today over eight pounds than you weel under eight," one of the guides drawls in musical Kiwi.

"That's right, mate," his buddy offers. "These are the ooonly trout that can run a six-foot eel out of the pool."

I consider the possibilities and look around nervously. My friend Lou Rago sidearms a flask in my direction. "Here," he says, "better have a swig." He knows I am an emotional mess and I'm not even on the water yet.

I make the final filtering of the Glenfiddich through the charcoal of a cigarette, almost swallowing the entire butt. Not bad. I think I'm ready. But Tim McCarthy, head guide at Tongariro Lodge, isn't so sure. He has drawn the long straw: he will be guiding Dick and me.

Why am I so nervous? I've landed forty-inch steelhead, haven't I? So has Larsen. So have a lot of us.

"It's a bit of a walk," McCarthy warns, looking mostly at me as we wait for the chopper. I suck my stomach in and square my shoulders.

"How long?" I ask.

"Fourteen kilometers."

"How many miles is that?"

"Eight and a half. Mostly boulders and some pretty nasty river bottom. We'll head cross-country if we have to. Mostly it's OK. Just a keen hike."

Larsen picks up his rod and exhales his $50 Esplendido. "Good shit," he says. "Nine for a five-weight, baby. That's the one. How's my drag?"

McCarthy looks at the reel, but mostly at our legs, and winces. Larsen and I have probably not walked eight and a half miles at any time in our lives. We both normally do our hiking in jet boats up in British Columbia.

"Ahh, those steelhead are fun all right, but it's a no-brainer," the first guide says, without apparent malice or contempt. He goes on in the same manner, smiling one of those smiles you begin to hate after you've passed fifty-five. "There are a lot of guests who couldn't make this hike," he says, looking at us.

Larsen is cool and shows no emotion, certainly not intimidation from a mere eight and a half-mile trek into the mouth of a feeding trout like those we are supposed to see today. But his veins are pounding. He steadies himself, leaning on his African walking stick—the one he got from a Masai warrior in trade for an empty 35-millimeter plastic film canister. The Masai like to use film canisters as functional earrings, filling them with miscellania and then inserting them into large holes in their lower ears.

Larsen hefts his end of the bargain in a cloud of aromatic Cuban fog. He taps the hiking stick against his legs and says, "Ironwood, baby." Which one? I ask myself. His leg or the stick?

Now it is 8:45 a.m. and we are flying up the main river canyon. From 900 feet, the semitropical forests of New Zealand's North Island drift below us, folded in images of green cauliflower-like foliage and crumpled canyons whose small tributaries still run in shadow and cold morning fog. Moss hangs from the limbs of some trees like strange, uncombed green hair. We could be in Cambodia, Laos, Borneo, or over the lush tangle of Hawaii. I see what appear to be red flowers and immense umbrella-shaped ferns.

This isn't Kansas, Toto. If half of what the guides say is true, the trout below really are unbelievable.

I have seen their smaller cousins to the south and west; two days earlier, on another branch of this same river, I cast to a brown estimated to weigh fourteen pounds. I saw a rainbow that looked every bit as large, and others that ranged in size from six to maybe twelve pounds. In one pool, forty casts produced two "looks" and thirty-eight "kiss-my-anal-fin" refusals, each more emphatic than the last, until finally all the trout were onto us, and ganged up in fifteen feet of water in the deepest part of the pool. As we left, Ken Drummond, a great guide and friend, counted more than a dozen of them.

Drummond always shortens my name and pronounces it as if it were spelled "Lawn," and the memory of his coaching brings a smile:

"A little to the left, Lawn."

"A littlc to thc right, Lawn."

"A little longer, Lawn."

"Oh, he's gone, Lawn."

Coaching helps. If you can take instruction, guiding and honest criticism, you will get it. New Zealand guides are perfectionists, superbly gifted and practiced anglers with eyes that can see everything—including your nerves, your ego, and every weakness you have as an angler, even those you try to hide. If you're smart, you check your privates on some tree by the gravel bar before you wade into position, although most Kiwi pros have apparently unlimited patience. But they will demand that you wear dark clothing, with no red hankies around the throat until the fish is in the net and the cameras are out of the bag. They also insist you have no chrome-plated tools dangling from a light-colored vest, and no wristwatches that might catch the sun and flash in the eye of a trout as long as your arm.

Some even apply steel wool or powdered pumice to their $900 fly rods to scour away the glossy finish. By doing so they reduce the chance of signaling to the trout that all is not well and that the airborne cicada making impossible turns at the speed of light is actually connected to the strange animal waving its arms back and forth over there on the rock.

Tim McCarthy even goes so far as to dye the sheepskin fly patch on his vest. He dyes it black. This is serious stuff.

Everything else is fairly typical. You bring three rods: a small creek rod of say, seven and a half feet, but you never use it, and maybe a nine and a half-foot six- or seven-weight for a poke at the lower Tongariro on the North Island or the Buller on the South, and the all-important ace in the hole: the nine-footer for a 5/6 weight line. But you don't bring flies. The guides usually won't let you use your own flies because their patterns have been field tested under conditions that can make our spring creek fishing back home look tame.

Add a few fourteen- to eighteen-foot leaders in 4X and 5X with fluorocarbon tippets, some yarn for indicators (white, yellow or green, but not red) and you're all set.

The water is relatively warm, usually in the high fifties in late summer, so waders are optional. Most cool hands show up in felt-soled wading shoes worn over a pair of polypropylene long johns and a pair of quick-drying hiking shorts.

We are now at 300 feet and the river begins to come into focus. It is beautiful beyond imagination. In the glare of sunlight it is silver, but one more turn and it yields to cerulean, then turquoise and finally the sweetest green you can imagine. It crawls in serpentine fashion through boulders and mossy canyons, then hangs like a necklace of jade in a myriad of fantastic stone settings, a pulsing artery, alive and shining. It is more than that; it is the most incredible piece of trout water I have seen in forty-five years of looking, and now—at 300 feet—at least one of its trout is suddenly visible. The heavy-shouldered monster lumbers away from the noise of the chopper and disappears into shadow. Do you know how large a trout has to be if you can see it from 300 feet?

We drop smoothly through an opening in the trees and the river explodes in circular waves from our rotors. The invasion from outer space has begun. Moments later, the Bell Jet leaves us there and leans south into oblivion like a howling insect. The wilderness gathers like a shroud.

We are here. All alone. The Inner Sanctum is ours.

Packs and gear are gathered, and I notice for the third time this morning that I have a guide with a walking stick. The first I've ever seen.

Larson grins, and fondles his ironwood. I reach around to see if the collapsible wading staff he lent me is still there.

Tim begins the instructions as we start walking. "We will not," he says emphatically, "fish right away, but will hike for two hours, no matter what we see. It's necessary. Otherwise we will never make the fourteen kilometers to the 6 p.m. pick-up and we'll have to stay all night."

This is the last day of our trip and I have a non-refundable $1,500 ticket and a more than decent wife waiting for me to come home. Nevertheless, the thought of staying all night and fishing one more day is tempting. After all, there are no bears here, no man-eating tigers, no snakes—not even any snake-oil salesmen disguised as timber-management specialists.

Besides, for all I know the mortgage payment is due at home. Not only that, while I have some pretty hefty trout written down somewhere in my notes—including a nine-pound rainbow yesterday—it would be nice to add a few more. Larsen has fared even better; he took a ten and a half-pound brown when we fished the South Island's "Wherearewe" River on a trek we affectionately referred to as the Death March of February 15, or simply "Camp Boris," named after the guide who dragged him and Washington, D.C. angler John Ferguson along several miles of secret pools where nothing was under ten pounds.

I watch Tim, who has now stopped and is waiting for us to catch up. He is looking at the center of a pool as we join him. He points. "Not bad," he grins. "Better than that, actually. About nine pounds.

A rainbow. But we can't stop. I know it's hard, but we're better off doing the bulk of our walking now than at the end of the day."

An hour later we are in the guts of it. The forest canopy here is spectacular—a thousand chandeliers of curling limbs, covered with moss coiling across a clear blue sky and cotton clouds. Leaves wet with last night's rain sparkle like diamonds in the sunlight. There are no cut stumps or man-made signs anywhere; the forest is still aboriginal, perfect and unspoiled. The ground is spongy and so rich it smells of peat. Immense ferns and small wildflowers hang suspended like intricate floral bouquets over water so clear that ten feet of depth looks like three, and four-foot boulders shrink to pebble size. It is cool and refreshing in the shade. When you ford the shallows on a crossing, swimming mayfly nymphs scurry erratically away from your boots, and the hollow ghosts of last month's stonefly hatch cling to rocks still drying in the sun.

Suddenly a deer whistles and the sound echoes through the forest. A fish rolls heavily in the pool just ahead, free and undisturbed. He has seen nobody in a month. It is one of those defining moments when the best expressions of the sport are palpable, within reach, and the river you are wading is full of wild trout that few anglers have seen, or caught. I expect to see monkeys or Munchkins, but none appear.

"This is incredible!" Larsen exclaims. "When do we meet Tyrannosaurus Rex?"

The first pool we will fish is just ahead now, shining in the light and Tim has a fish spotted.

"It isn't a really big one," he says, "but a good place to start—about seven pounds. Who's up first?"

It's a complicated issue and Larsen and I think about it. The run looks like an easy shot. The currents coming in at the head are straight; drag will not be an issue. A high cliff borders the river on the right and Tim says the fish is feeding heavily in the center current like a phantom submarine, gliding back and forth ingesting who knows what. Maybe caddis. The cast will be forty feet from a position directly below the fish and the tailout is a broad sweeping fan of shallow water with no trees near; there's plenty of room for a backcast.

I look at the run. It seems incandescent in the morning light. The tailout is still in shadow. The caster will be hidden. Perfect. I can't see the trout.

So, the first pool is always a mixed bag. On one hand, you're wired and ready for the big tug. On the other, you've been sweating and walking for so long you'd rather just flop down in the moss and take five. The thought also crosses my mind that what I really wanted to do was just get in the water, open my mouth and let the entire river run into my stomach. But I also had a down-in-my-gut, gnawing feeling that I really didn't want to be the first one of the day to blow a fish and a hard-earned opportunity. Not after two hours of hiking. If I let the other guy do that, then somehow it seems like my own sins on the next pool and for the rest of the day are somehow diminished by his.

I wonder if Larsen feels the same way. During this trip he has qualified for induction into my own pantheon of angling heroes, not only by delivering some of the best jokes I've ever heard, but also for a piece of wisdom that will change my life forever.

"Do you know," he asked while I was crawling over a fallen log, "What the single most important factor is for good health and longevity?"

I was swimming in sweat and fantasizing about a root-beer float. "Exercise?" I asked.

"Nope."

"Diet?"

"Uh-uh."

"No booze, or ciggies?"

"Nah."

"Well, what is it then?"

"Flossing your teeth."

"Larsen, come on."

"No, it's true. Your immune system has to work very hard cleaning the germs out of your teeth and gums. The effort doesn't leave much in reserve for defense against attacks on other fronts. So if you help out on the gummy end of things, you can live to be at least ninety-five. No matter what else you do." He gestured with the Masai stick to punctuate the comment.

That was almost enough, but the clincher came later while we were waiting in the Auckland airport for the long ride home. We had checked our voicemail and compared numbers of messages (the "How many do you have?" game.)

"Three hundred and seventy," Larsen said.

"Whaat?"

"Three hundred and seventy."

He wasn't kidding.

Then, three hours later, as the milling throng of international passengers started fighting one another for early boarding and the best shot at an overhead luggage compartment close to their seats, Larsen put on his shades, ruffled his hair and started leaning a bit, listing seriously to port. He looked weak and confused. Suddenly, without warning, he moved forward in a meandering, staggering path, tapping his Masai cane back and forth on the floor as if he were blind, alone and afraid. The rest of us watched incredulously as two airline attendants sprang to his side to help him tap his way past the business-class passengers, past the old lady in a wheelchair, past all the first-class passengers waiting to board.

Forty minutes later, when I got on the plane, Larsen was already asleep. The Masai stick was safely stored in the overhead luggage compartment above his seat.

My reverie is broken as Tim asks again, "Who's up?"

"Waller is," Larsen says generously, and I can hear the sound echoing off the canyon walls and reverberating all the way back to the lodge where I feel like everyone is watching us on television—to say nothing of Tim McCarthy, ace guide and expert trouter, who is now crouched in the bushes waiting for first blood by a guy who writes stories and performs in videos.

My first cast is short. That's all right, it usually is. After all, you don't want to line the darn thing.

The next one is six feet to the left (sudden breeze) and the fly lands in three inches of water. I have no idea where the fish is because I can't see it in the glare.

"Do you see him?" Tim asks.

"Yeah, I've got him," I shout back.

My next cast is eight feet to the right and almost lands on the rocky outcrop (sudden lack of breeze.)

"Are you sure you see him?" Tim asks.

"Well, I'm not sure, I guess. Where is he?" All I can see is ten million rocks at the bottom of the river and an endless labyrinth of forest.

"Do you see the brown rock?"

"Which one?"

"The one by the green bush."

"Which green bush?"

"The one by the tree."

"Oh, yeaaah..."

"Well, come straight out from the brown rock for ten feet. Then go four feet up to the gray boulder and then seven feet to the side. Then drop back a foot. He's just to the right of the fourth tan rock. The one next to the one that's not quite so tan."

Then, suddenly, I see him. The next cast is perfect and I watch the shiny leader turn over in the sun, flashing (not a good thing, but what the hell, it's out there isn't it?), then settling gently to the water. The cicada indicator dry fly drifts down with the size eighteen Passenger Caddis Nymph tied on 5x tippet following closely behind. I wonder which one he'll take. He's just to the side of the rock, over there by the shadow. I see him. He's lifting, and I'm ready to hit him.

Then Tim stands and makes the reel-'em-up gesture with his right hand.

"What's going on?" I ask.

"Your cast was ten feet too long. He's gone. You lined him. I told you he was by the brown rock, next to the green bush."

The next trout took only ten minutes to find. A large fish rose with a shouldering splash just at the head of a shallow pool, in full sunlight next to a drop-off where the water ran like lime soda. Then a second trout surged on the other side, rolling over small cobblestones with the weight of his body, blowing open a muddy hole in the riffle as he turned to collect his harvest of nymphs. He was so big I instinctively thought "steelhead."

This time Larsen was up, thank God. He was already in position and maneuvering to attack, apparently with nerves of steel, his head and shoulders invisible in a cloud of cigar smoke as he puffed and double-hauled at the same time.

I wondered how he could see anything. He had no head, legs or torso—just arms. Four feet of gin-clear water and his fuming Cuban had erased everything else. Each haul and each puff added another five feet to the length of line he had in the air until I thought he would line these two fish and have a decent shot at one in the next pool upstream.

"NOW!" Tim shouted.

I didn't see what happened when he let go of the cast. The polarizing filter for my camera had fallen down inside my waders and I had to urinate. When I looked up again, Larsen was reeling in and there was nothing on the end of his line. I think he shrugged, but I couldn't be sure; there was so much smoke out there.

Later, while we were eating lunch, I got to thinking about Tim and everything he had to go through to make his living. I had to ask.

"Tim?"

"Yeah?"

"Do you have the same nightmare every night, with only the faces changing?"

"You're close."

"What changes?"

"The boot size."

At $600 a day U.S., fishing success or failure becomes a serious business—not so much because of economics (who gives a damn? it's only money) but because of ego and because the hour is growing late and this could be it for another year. That's the stuff of nightmares.

So that afternoon, after lunch, old Larsen and I did our best to help Tim get a good night's sleep. But after eight more pools, twenty-seven fly changes over ten truly large fish that refused fifty decent presentations, and six more kilometers of walking, I no longer gave a shit who hooked one of the bastards, as long as one of us did. The bigger the better.

How about a twenty-pounder? They were in here, weren't they?

I guess the same idea hit Dick about the time his third Esplendido wore out. We started walking closer together and talking. Now that I think about it, maybe the conversation meant more than our fishing. All I knew then was that we had walked a very long way and made dozens of casts without a strike.

A half hour later, when it was my turn to be up again, I went for it, hip-deep in water, with my life and reputation fully exposed, trying my best to just make it, just make the frigging cast. Everything else could go to hell.

Are you kidding? There was nothing else.

I knew the fish was a good one because Tim hadn't said anything about its size. I was nervous enough already. Even at forty feet, and from a crouched position, I could see the trout moving back and forth like a fighter plane, gliding up and down in currents as clear as air while I just tried to keep from falling down and drowning in its liquid sky.

He or she swam from right to left, then right again, then up and over a rock that went in and out of focus as I prayed for no wind and a good loop. The trout looked like a chinook salmon, all shoulders and heavy flanks. It looked black in the clear water and for a moment I thought Tim had blown it and I was casting to the fattest eel in New Zealand.

I made the cast, several in fact, but they weren't quite right and my would-be trophy would have none of it. When we left the pool, Tim looked away. "Too bad," he offered. "That was a nice one. You didn't do anything wrong." But I knew better.

"How big?" I asked.

"Maybe twelve or thirteen. A brown."

On Dick's next turn, we cut through a shrubby plateau to find Tim down on his knees, staring at the river. He asked me if I had seen the big brown at the head of the pool. I looked, and if I fish another seventy years I won't forget what I saw. I'm not embarrassed to admit that I had seen it even before he pointed it out, but I thought it was a log.

Three smaller fish lay just downstream from the log—one a rainbow of perhaps eleven pounds and a couple of others that appeared to be around eight or nine.

"The brown might go seventeen or more," Tim whispered. "I have heard of twenty-pounders being taken from this section of river." Then he turned his attention to Larsen and me. "Who's up?" he asked.

Larsen had one eye on me, the other on the huge brown. "Have you ever taken a really big one?" he asked.

"No."

"Go get 'im. He's yours."

"Dick, it isn't my turn. I had the last shot."

"Shut up. Take him. I've got mine."

By this time the brown had turned and was lumbering slowly back down to the tailout. As he passed us I could see his body and his eye. He looked like a brooding shark with the head of a trout. When he took up a new position just above the riffle below the tailout, I began crawling toward him on my hands and knees, praying as I did so.

The forty-five-foot crawling stalk under the cover of forest shadows took fifteen minutes. The casting took a lot less. I had five refusals on five presentations. My five-weight line and .005-inch leader tippet looked like rope in the sun. I did manage three fantasies about taking casting lessons as soon as I returned to California and one promise to never say "fuck" again in public if the damn thing would just bite.

After the fifth cast, I was out of tricks. Tim motioned for me to crawl back up toward the head of the pool. "It's no use, he knows we're here," he said. "Try those rainbow over there." Larsen nodded approval, pointing at one with his ironwood stick.

I turned for a last look for the brown. It was gone. It hadn't taken, so there was no point keeping my promise about vocabulary. "Fuck him," I said to myself.

Then I changed focus to the rainbows at the head of the pool. The cast looked impossible because there were trees right behind me. The only possibility was to make a twenty-foot backcast almost straight up in the air, then shoot a perfectly straight cast forty feet over the rainbows to a spot about the size of a large serving platter, then mend quickly to avoid drag.

Somehow I made it. The shot was perfect and the fly hit just right, the way they can sometimes. Even Tim liked the cast.

And wouldn't you know? One of those magnificent rainbows saw the fly and quivered. Six desperate human eyes watched intently as the size 14 Royal Wulff wiggled its butt in the meniscus and passed over the trout like a little red ship with white sails. Just for a second I felt like a hero, but then I mended too late and drag set in. The trout dropped to the bottom.

Larsen motioned for me to try the other fish, and my next shot was fired at the big rainbow near the top of the pool. He was twenty feet away and feeding in plain sight and there were no trees anywhere nearby and the wind was perfect, coming in over my left shoulder. It was an easy shot at the trout of a lifetime and I blew the cast so badly that Larsen cleared his throat behind me and Tim just looked at the ground and said nothing.

Finally we reached the last pool of the day—and the trip and the year. Darkness was falling and we'd been walking all day. A ragged brown nymph was hooked in the second snake guide just down from the tip-top of my rod and I reached for it with an odd feeling. 5:30 p.m. This was it, the last chance.

Fatigue and paranoia gathered. I hadn't had a strike all day. I had, however, just fallen in on the last crossing, soaking my Nikon and my ego. I was cold and on edge.

What a way to end it, I thought, shivering. Not one strike.

I wondered what Tim thought of me. And what about Larsen?

The fly was loose from the snake guide and Tim was back at his post, watching like a heron as he had all day, never quitting, never giving up, never showing a sign of impatience or urgency. Larsen is waiting patiently, too, sitting on a sandy bank in the dark shade of wonderful trees and clutching his Masai stick. He is here for the same reason I am: He loves it.

As for me, I'm just a little older and a little tired. But maybe I'm ready for this one.

Tim begins his work. The fish looks good, he says, and she's lying only two feet from an almost sheer wall of lemon-colored stone to my right and up forty feet. Just there by the cut with marbled streaks of black on it.

I look. The water is purple over there. I'll never see her.

"She's feeding heavily," Tim cautions. He says nothing of her size, but it doesn't matter. I've done all I can and the guy back at the lodge was right; I'd rather be skunked here than land twenty in a no-brainer somewhere else.

The line unrolls in the air and I refuse to let it go until I have those words jammed down into the rod and reel and anywhere else I can stick them because they are the truth. Finally I let it go, all thirty feet of it plus fifteen feet of leader and it looks really good as it unfolds in the cooling air like a beautiful arrow going straight to the heart of something I can't explain, but can't live without.

"Grrreat shot," Tim whispers. "Let it go, let it go. Oh-oh, wait a minute, she's moved upstream now about five feet and she's right up against the wall. Right next to it. Pick it up and go again. Now!" (They always say that.)

The cast is now fifty-five feet and the fly has to land a foot from the cliff wall or she might not see it. The line lifts off the water like oil, smooth and sweet behind me, and I am begging my wrist and arm to wait and get it right, and I pull just enough with my line hand to gain another ten feet. I've been doing this for fifty years; when will it become automatic, without anxiety and prayers for luck?

When everything lands out there the indicator is almost kissing the rock. But is the leader straight? Where is the fly?

"Perfect," Tim whispers.

Nothing happens for ten years. Then without warning Tim is screaming: "LIFT! DAMMIT, LIFT!"

I look at the indicator. What's this lift stuff? What's he talking about? The indicator hasn't twitched; the drift is as steady as silk, smooth and certain. But I know this: I'm lifting, pal. This guy knows what he's talking about.

I raise the rod and the fish is there. I greet her with another private, very happy vulgarity. I have her. She's on!

I'm not very good at describing fish fights. I wish I were because this one was a beauty. I saw her sailing through canyons of deep water with the light reflecting from her sides and I bit my lip when she shook the line like a dog. I ran downstream and then back upstream four or five times with all the grace of a wounded ostrich, holding my rod up high and winding the reel with my back to the fish so I could see where I was going, and not trip again.

But it was the jumps I most remember. When she came out, she seemed to hang in the air over the dark water like a great balloon, beautiful and silver as the morning sky, and when I saw her girth I didn't think it was possible for a stream resident rainbow trout to grow that large. Not even in New Zealand.

And I remember the look on Tim's face as she finally came on her side into the shallows.

"God, what a horse," he whispered.

Even Larsen was impressed and said something like "Holy shit." Actually, that's exactly what he said and I silently thanked him for the perfect description, because when you get right down to it we are not really vulgar. We are not liars. We're just informal descriptionists.

And then she was in the net, straining against the cord, with her wet tail flopping in the air. She looked like a salmon and I loved her instantly.

Tim whistled as the arrow steadied on the scale. "Thirteen pounds," he gasped excitedly. "A female. What a fatso. That's the biggest trout I've ever landed with a client on any river I've fished." His passion is genuine and threatens to expand my already burgeoning testicles, but the feeling doesn't last long. I couldn't help remembering the rest of the day and all my mistakes.

"How did you know she had taken?" I asked finally. "I didn't see the yarn hesitate."

"It didn't. I saw her lift in the water column. When she peaked I could see her white mouth open. I knew she had it."

Not long after—about fifteen minutes, I guess—and thirty feet around the next curving arc of river, Larsen dropped the last cast of the year on the nose of another humdinger. But he had to fight it without witnesses. That's because I was in a reverie, wandering around on the beach, still trying to find my missing polarizing lens, while Tim was busy writing notes about the thirteen-pounder.

Four times we heard Dick say "I think he's ready, get the net," and four times neither of us responded. Finally he gave up, landed the fish without help and held it as I showed up to get his photo.

My hands are still shaking. I look through the lens at Larsen. He hasn't shaved in ten days. He is not the prominent Washington, D.C., attorney who calls the President by his first name. Not any more. He's a bum. Or a scarecrow. Or a lion.

And so am I. We've been out for almost two blessed weeks. There are weeds and other dirty-looking things stuck to our shirts. Some look like bat droppings. But I don't give a damn, because in the past few minutes the two of us have held a total of nineteen pounds of perfectly formed rainbow trout in our hands, and right now at least, that's all that really matters, isn't it?

This is our reward for eight and a half miles of inhalations and exhalations, for legs that are beginning to cramp, for arms bleeding from bush cuts and sore from endless casting to the mythic shapes of magic trout hanging like torpedoes in water as clear as air, and as I take a final look through the lens I see the white flash of Larsen's flossed teeth. He's holding his Masai walking stick and grinning. "Ironwood, baby" he says. "Ironwood."

Day of the Manatee

It was 7:00 in the morning. Phil, my fishing buddy for the week, was taking no chances on a blazing Belizean sun. Standing in the bow like a spaniel on point, he was dressed neatly from neck to toe in his best sandy-tan bonefish scrubs. His head, at least what I could see of it, was enclosed in a beige-colored long-billed cap with a trailing cape that looked as if it belonged in the African desert. The French Foreign Legion would be proud. His hands were covered by anti-sun leather casting gloves; only the tips of his fingers were exposed. Everything else was covered, even his eyes. They remained hidden behind polaroid darkness.

But the guy could see.

He also had a $1,600 reel built by Jack Charleton. When I turned it, each revolution felt like the tumbler of an expensive safe, and it made me green with envy. I'd often thought I should just steal it, though I knew I'd have trouble removing his name, which was tooled on the drag plate.

The reel was attached to the end of a $700 graphite tarpon rod with a Portuguese cork fighting grip and a reel seat resembling the drive shaft on a Formula One racing car. Phil, as always was the quintessentially well-equipped fly fisher.

Phil is a one layer man and wears no shorts when he fishes in tropical settings and when he casts, it is impossible not to notice. One could argue that the image is similar to the documentary in which the hippo tries to climb up the bank to have a shot at a cool place in the shade. I closed my eyes, replacing one image with another—the gleaming plates and rattling gills of an air-borne tarpon over one hundred and fifty pounds.

"This is the day," he said suddenly, turning around. "We're gonna drill 'em. Wanna beer?"

"Yeah, OK. What time is it?"

"7:30. You ready?"

"Yeah, I'm ready. Whaddya wanna do?"

"I dunno. Let's ask Martin."

Martin, our trusty guide, was in the back of the boat getting organized, sliding his cushion around, picking some tarpon flies up off the carpet, blowing his nose, smelling the wind, cleaning his glasses and looking at the two dudes in front of him.

In contrast to Phil, I was half-naked. My shorts were too short and tight and I didn't know why. They had looked all right when I bought them. Only a few years ago. Maybe they shrank. And how in the hell had my belly gotten so far over the edge of my custom-made bonefish belt? I had no shoes on, my cotton shirt was crumpled and rolled up past skinny elbows that looked like chicken wings. My legs were even worse. And I'd forgotten my fishing outfit. The hippo it seems had found the perfect companion.

"I 'gotta' get my gear" I said.

Phil nodded in agreement and I went to find my equipment, running a tropical gauntlet of starving mosquitoes all the way back to the lodge. Rushing into our room, I almost punched an eye out on the tip of my tarpon rod, which was leaning against the side of my bed. Even inside the air was full of mosquitoes. The front porch smelled sweetly of orchids. I had to use the bathroom. Badly.

But it would have to wait. I rushed back to the boat, almost ready at last—and always, it seemed, the last ready. I have, over the years, considered the possibility that my tardiness, even when fishing, is because I have additional responsibilities, including, but not limited to the continual urge to write screen plays and songs as I go about my daily routine, the interminable desire to illuminate the basic condition of mankind through an absolutely brilliant manifesto and to decide once and for all, if I should have groped Betty Simpson at the senior prom some forty four years ago. In truth however, none of these possibilities seem adequate explanations. I am simply disorganized.

"You ready now, Waller?"

"Yup. What did you decide to do?"

"Go for tarpon. What else?"

The flats beyond the estuarial mouth of the Belize River form a broad expanse of shimmering water, dancing with choppy little tea-colored waves, although the river itself comes in green. Pushing a warm flood of sweet water into the waiting mouth of the bay, the river, brown and roily, eventually mixes with the sea, with the speed of the process depending on rainfall and tides. Yesterday, as we returned to camp in a dusky orange evening light, I had seen the line where fresh and saltwater met. It looked good.

"You want to hit the river or the flats?" I asked Phil.

"The flats. Martin says there are some big ones out there where the freshwater meets the salt. They'll be in four feet of water now with the tides the way they are and we have good light. Lets look for some. Besides, we didn't get anything really big yesterday in the river, did we?"

"OK. Sounds good."

Martin grinned. "We'll get them," he said. "There are some big boys in there now. I spotted them a week ago and they're still there. Some are well over 100 pounds. There are always about fifty or sixty of them and I think they live there. I always see them when the tides and light are the way they are now."

Phil turned the handle of his reel, looked at me and smiled.

Belizean tarpon are significantly smaller on average than those found in Florida. Tarpon in the saltwater "cricks," channels and lagoons of Belize usually go anywhere from twenty to eighty pounds—certainly smaller than the monsters of Homosassa, but good nonetheless. Decent fish. Now and then you get a shot at one even bigger, big enough for anyone. I've seen a few near 150 or even 170 pounds.

The river tarpon, appropriately called "baby tarpon," run from shad size to maybe eighty pounds or so—if you're lucky. But whether in rivers or saltwater, all seem susceptible to bright fly patterns. Belizean guides swear by orange and yellow or red and white.

"Who's up?" Martin asked, cutting the motor. "You better be ready. We can see them at any time." He let the boat drift into place and took the pole in his hands, ready to go.

I still wasn't ready. I didn't like my line and wanted to change it. "You go," I told Phil. "I have to change my line."

"What kind you got on?" Martin asked, sticking the pole deep in sandy silt and leaning forward to see.

"I've got an intermediate."

"What do you have?" he asked Phil.

"Same."

"It's better to have a fast sinker on one rod and a floater on the other. There are some deeper holes around the channel up ahead that we'll blind cast into, and I want you down in those. We can use the floater when we're in shallow water and can spot them."

I sat down and pulled the intermediate off the spool of my reel while Phil got up on the casting platform. His 3/0 fly was red and white. Martin turned to me and said, "Put on a 'Roach. No, wait a minute. Get the biggest orange and yellow you have."

The 6/0 orange and yellow fly emerged from the stretcher box like a psychedelic condor. The wings stuck out at a forty-five-degree angle. It looked like a small airplane. It was almost as big as my hand.

"Perfect," Martin said.

He pushed again and the heavy panga moved forward quickly. The light was at our back and the breeze rippled our shirts. The water was as tan as Phil but we could see through it with our polaroid glasses and for the next twenty minutes we searched for fish. They look like floating logs in water like that, suspended near the surface, and they can come upon you almost before you know it. Then it's all about speed and staying cool—two of my least reliable responses.

Phil's trousers were flapping in the breeze as I handed him another Belikan beer, the Belizean favorite. His amber nylon sounded like it would rip in the wind.

"Where did you get those clothes?" I asked. "You look like a camel."

"I wouldn't talk if I were you," he replied. "I can't even see your belt. Besides, who's caught the only tarpon so far? Not only that, but how did you like the way it jumped. Pretty nifty, eh?"

He was on a roll. "In fact, how many fish did you catch before we came here?" he asked pointedly. "We've been down here for a week and a half and I'll tell you what you caught at the last place: One measly bonefish about sixteen inches. That's all. Not only that, you caught it blind casting into a pile of mudding fish. What kind of trips do you run, anyway?"

"Dammit, Phil," I said. "The brochure looked good. And anyway, we're doing a lot better here, aren't we? I know I haven't caught much, but if Jerry were here, I'd at least be ahead of him. What's he doing anyway? Why didn't he come with us?"

"He's opening a new fly shop in Phoenix. Only the best. Custom-wrapped rods with jungle-cock inserts laminated next to the hook keeper, and some new tool he invented. Gonna make him rich, he says."

"What's that?"

"A pair of pliers with serrated, lifetime carbide jaws that telescope out into a nymph net for collecting insect samples. It has a built-in flashlight and compass on one side and a map of Alaska on the other in case you're ever up there and get lost. Or you can just call, because it ties into a cellular phone. I'm gonna get one because. . . ."

"Now!" Martin screamed suddenly. "Now! One o'clock and eighty feet away. Coming fast! Coming fast! Two of them. Do you have them? Do you have them?"

We had them. They looked brown, long and snaky in the water, moving without apparent effort, almost as if they were gliding in air. They were indeed coming fast. One of them would go 100 pounds, the other around seventy-five.

"I see them," Phil said.

"Wait. Wait until I say go," Martin commanded. "Then go fast. You'll only get one shot. They're not too happy and are moving fast, traveling, but you'll get the shot. You'll get the shot." He turned the boat sideways, giving Phil the room needed for a backcast.

The tarpon seemed to be moving in slow motion; yet they were coming as fast as a train, just under the surface, heading right for us. When I'm excited, which is all the time when I'm fishing or watching someone else fish, the targets always look twice the size they really are and I held my breath as Phil gave it to them.

The cast was long, just to the back and behind the large one. They were now twenty feet away, on the brink of bolting.

"Pick it up, pick it up, go again, go again now!" Martin whispered, but it was no use. The tarpon had seen us. They did nothing visible, they just vanished. In four feet of water. Only ten feet from the gunnel. I don't know how they did it.

"Dammit, I'm sorry," Phil said.

"Not your fault," Martin answered. "You didn't get a good shot. They were coming in too fast, that's all. It happens."

"Don't worry, Phil," I added. "Those fish were uncatchable."

"Think so? Do you really think so?"

"Hell, yes."

He grinned. "Let's re-book for next year as soon as we get back to camp."

Now it was my turn, and I was finally ready. I stood on the casting platform for twenty minutes while nothing happened. We were over deeper water now.

Something went by, a dark shadow as large as a tree. "Manatee," Martin said. It passed like a submarine, strong and silent. Straining to see it, I almost fell from the casting platform.

The wind was stronger now, coming from the south, blowing clouds that looked like pieces of soft cotton across a turquoise-colored sky. I stepped down to the deck where it was easier to stand up in the wind.

It was the last afternoon of the trip, and I was tired as hell.

"Yeah, I'm having a good time, all right," Phil said. "Let's see . . . how much has this cost us so far?"

"With or without air fare?"

"Without."

"Well, hang on," I said, mentally calculating. "Let's see. We paid $2,500 for the lodge last week, and about $100 for the permit flies, plus tips for the guides, plus the carved ebony whales and lodge shirts."

"What about our bar bill?"

"$700, but I figure those other guys must have put some of theirs on ours."

"Probably."

"What did we pay here?"

"About $1,200 for the lodge, plus tips, our bar bill and the coconut ashtrays. Not only that, but we. . . ."

"Here he is, here he is!" Martin shouted. "Nine o'clock and laid up about 100 feet away! Another good one! Do you see him? Do you see him?"

"I've got 'im! I've got 'im!" I shouted enthusiastically, squinting through the combination of sweat and insect repellent that was draining into my eyes.

The tarpon looked happy. It moved a little to its left, then stopped and turned to its right, looking, then started cruising slowly right at me. It looked as big as an African rhino.

This should be easy, I thought. The shot will be at 9:30 or maybe 9:00. And I'm right handed. Perfect. Slow and steady.

The rod rolled forward and the line left the tip in an airborne loop I couldn't see but I was certain it would be the cast of a lifetime. "Wait till Phil sees this," I thought. The line straightened in front, then reversed into an invisible back cast as the tarpon approached fifty feet.

"Shoot it now," Martin whispered. "He's about ninety pounds."

The line unfolded in the air, somewhere over my right shoulder, the green taper apparently going exactly where it was supposed to go. "Magnificent," I muttered to myself. Then the line came forward again, entering my vision and dropping like a bomb, landing in a pile twenty feet behind the tarpon and twenty feet to the wrong side. Phil sat down.

"Go again, go again," Martin urged softly. "Hurry, hurry! Pick it up, pick it up!"

I don't remember much after that, except for the strike. My second cast, all fifteen feet of it, dropped somewhere out in the general vicinity of where I was aiming. I guess the tarpon didn't see the fly, but he must have heard it. I do remember seeing the fly floating all alone in the ocean, looking like an orange chicken lost at sea while I stood there staring at the tarpon. The fish turned from side to side, searching for whatever it had heard or sensed striking the water, then lunged toward the fly and took it with an explosion of swirling water. I can still see the open gills with light coming through the rakers as it inhaled the 6/0 orange and yellow fly, shook its head like a dog with a rat, then turned and ripped off forty yards of line so quickly it tangled and then passed through the guides in a knot as large as a Florida orange.

"Oh, no!" Phil said. "Here, want my reel? We can tie it to yours."

Somehow, despite the tangle, I survived the first four jumps. Then, after the tarpon had settled down, Martin came to my side and miraculously freed the orange knot. After that the fight slugged on, and at one point I heard Phil's voice behind me: "God, he's pulling the boat."

And so he was, but one hour, two beers and three strawberry sodas later, just when I thought I had him, I finally tightened the drag a little too much and the class tippet broke when the fish made a final lunge with strength I thought it no longer had. It disappeared into the green water, a long shadow never to be seen again.

"Jeez, that's too bad," Martin said. "But you had a good fight, anyway. What the hell. Not only that, but how many bonefish would you say we've taken since you got here?" he asked, trying hard to find the bright side. "You've fished bones for three days."

"About eighty," I estimated, starting on another strawberry soda. "What do you think, Phil?"

"About that, I'd guess."

"Let me check," Martin said. "I have it written down." He consulted a notebook, but the answer wasn't forthcoming right away.

"Well, how many?" Phil asked finally, leaning into the question like a heron on the mudflats of San Francisco Bay.

"Twenty-two," Martin said.

By then the day was well spent and Phil and I both knew our tarpon fishing was almost over for another year. I could see he was considering putting his gear away. The heat was past and the windows of Belize City reflected the setting sun like a string of diamonds nestled among the palms and mangroves. I reeled in, ready for the ride back and one last Belikan, but Martin was never one to quit.

"Hey, I know one more place where we might get one," he said. "Let's give it a shot for a few minutes. Do you still have the sinking lines handy"?

We both replied in the affirmative.

The chosen place was a circular hole about twelve feet deep, scalloped by tidal flow from a soft mixture of sand, dead coral and mud. It was only a hundred yards from the waterfront lots of an abandoned community building project. Martin said the project had been financed by a group of Hong Kong investors who failed to do their homework, and when the first buildings began sinking into the mud the whole thing had to be abandoned.

Some of the buildings appeared eight or nine stories high. They leaned at impossible angles with their bottom stories now underground. The sun was behind them, low on the horizon but still orange and bright, shining through broken windows and open doorways.

"Anybody still live there?" Phil asked.

"Nope," Martin said. "Why"?

"Oh, I dunno. Maybe we could open a lodge. Jerry could come down and do his shop thing here. We could even come out with our own line of equipment. Jungle Cock Salt Water Rods. Has a nice ring." He turned to me, smiling. "Would you book it, Waller?"

"How much commission? I usually get twenty percent."

"Five percent."

"Hell, yes. With tarpon fishing like this, my wife could even come down here and teach school. Have the houses stopped sinking yet?"

"Nope."

Martin rammed his pole into the mud and tied off the panga. Stirred by a tropical breeze and flood tide, the boat swiveled on its tether, giving Phil a perfect shot toward the building project's now-defunct pharmacia. My line of fire was to be the abandoned front lawn of a five-story condo lying halfway on its side.

"You boys are good enough to both fish at the same time," Martin said. "One in the middle and one from the bow. The tarpon can be anywhere. I poled us into the middle of the hole. We are right on top of them, and this is where the big boys come at night to feed. You can't miss."

Then he thought of something else. "Sometimes the manatees come in here to feed," he said. "But they stay away from the tarpon and they don't eat anything like the flies you boys are using, so don't worry."

We both started casting. I was using a thirty-foot extra-fast-sinking head connected to the supposedly tangleproof orange monofilament line I'd had on earlier when I hooked the tarpon. As it sailed toward the third story of the target condo, I could see it had a dogleg bend and a kinky spiral left over from the fight with the tarpon. It tried to maintain both as I began to retrieve.

I can't remember exactly, but I think it was the fifth or sixth cast when everything stopped and I pulled hard. The line held fast for a moment, then came free.

"Maybe the bottom," Phil suggested. "What's your count?"

He meant how many seconds I'd waited for the line to sink. "Fourteen," I said. "That should be about right for this density of line in twelve feet of water and a tide like we have now."

We both cast again. This time I counted only to ten, then started my retrieve. The line stopped again in the same place and I struck as hard as I could. Something out in the darkness pulled back like a car and there was a great explosion of mud all around the boat.

"Oh, God," I yelled, "I've got him!" My shooting line jumped off the deck and Martin had the anchor up before I knew it. We were off.

"Did you see the size of the boil and splash he made?" Martin asked. "This is the big one, all right, and you have him."

My line entered the water at a forty-five-degree angle and disappeared in the darkness. Something continued to pull hard at the other end. There was no head shaking or lurching, only a continuous strain and the quiet swimming of what felt like the largest thing I'd ever hooked.

After ten minutes it hit me: What if I'd hooked a manatee? Martin said they could be out there, in all that black water, sucking around the bottom.

"Martin," I said, "this thing is so big I can't hold it. And it's swimming funny. Listen, how big are manatees? What if I've hooked one?"

"It isn't a manatee. I know it."

The line sliced ahead, straining through the black tide. The panga followed like a barge being towed after the invisible monster swimming through the night.

"How do you know it isn't a manatee?" I asked, because I wanted to believe him. Maybe it was a world-record tarpon, hooked in front of an abandoned pharmacia and the third story of a leaning condo without windows. What a story.

"Because manatee don't jump!" Martin said. "I'm telling you, they just don't jump. Did you see the size of the splash he made right after you hooked him? It's a tarpon all right, a huge tarpon—maybe in the 200-pound class. They are here. I've seen a few bigger than that."

Euphoria. "Phil, baby," I shouted into the wind, "If I land it, and I'm going to, I'm 'gonna share the money with you. I have Mason tippet on. They'll pay a fortune for the photo."

For forty minutes the boat plowed on, and me with it, happily fantasizing about the glare of camera flashes from Belizean newspaper photographers who would gather at the dock when Martin called. All the kinks and doglegs had come out of my line, removed by the tremendous strain, and I felt the fight was starting to go my way.

Another half hour passed and finally a great form came slowly to the surface, unflinching and stubborn, as big as a cow, and at last we knew the truth: I had indeed hooked a manatee. I could see the execs at Mason, turning away and dissolving into the black sky.

Next morning, as we flew out of Belize City, I was seated next to a sweet, very petite lady in her late 70s who had come with her church group to "see the landscapes and all the beautiful wildlife they have down here."

"I saw a jaguar, you know, and so many wonderful flowers, the ruins of Altun Ha, and of all things, even a family of manatees!" she said. "The mother and baby were so cute, I just loved them to death. Have you ever seen one?"

I looked out the window at clouds that make me think of Felix the Cat and Porky Pig dancing arm-in-arm. A pod of tarpon swam nearby; one peeled off and came to a 'Roach, as it flanked Felix, then leaped in the sun. Not far behind, wrapped in another cloud, was a manatee, trailing a leader and a large orange fly. My God, I thought. Bovine. Jesus...Websters defines that as "cow like." I looked but couldn't see where the leader was coming from. What if I had hooked it in the teat? I wondered if the hook would ever rust out.

I turned back to the little old lady. "I saw a manatee myself, ma'am," I said, "but only for a moment, a little after sunset. It was going away and we were trying to catch up with it, so we could get a photo, but we never did."

"That's too bad," she said. "What wonderful swimmers they are. My guide told me they are very intelligent and quite sensitive. Some people say they mate for life. They remind me of dolphin or something, but I don't think they can jump like that, do you?"

"No, ma'am" I told her. "I don't think they can."

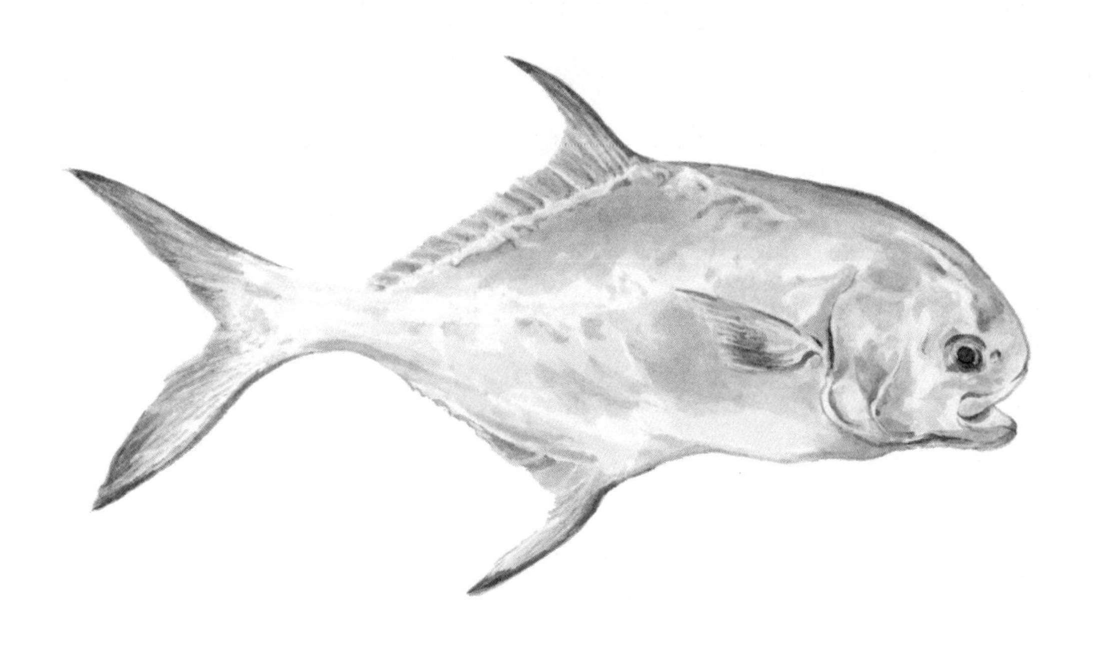

Scruffy the Cat

November 2, 1998

Dear Jack,

I'm sorry I haven't written sooner. I've been gone almost constantly since last spring when I left for the Bahamas with some friends to do some April bonefishing which was the beginning of my fishing this year. April is a good month for big bonefish if you hit it right and we look for them as they come swimming in with the early morning tides. The water is extraordinary then—blue, green and silver at the same time, tangerine or blood-red in the sunrise, and somehow still as clear as the air.

We fish in shallow places, sometimes weedy and crowded with saltwater grasses that curl away from the incoming tide. It's called turtle grass and the reason for the name is obvious, although you never see turtles in the shallows, only in deeper water and not often at all any more. The grass always points ahead to the fish, as bonefish like to swim into the tide and the wind, rooting like pigs in the sand and mud for small crabs, which they love, or for shrimp and whatever else they can find to eat. Sometimes we fish over barren sand and under the cry of ocean birds which I always think is a good sign, but there isn't much there for fish to eat that I can see. The fish seem to like it, though, and you can find them there.

I know you have always wanted to know why fisherman are the way they are, or why I go to all this trouble about it, but it's not easy to explain. Earlier this summer I was fishing in a jungle river not far outside Belize City, very near the wilderness which really is most of interior Belize. The Mayan ruins of Altun Ha are not far from the river, and I have seen them at dusk after a day of fishing. The stone pyramids are red from the setting sun at that time, and their carved gargolian heads still guard the temple 2,000 years after they were set in place. It's a wild spot. The cats, jaguar and ocelot, are still there, but they are nocturnal and quiet and you won't see them often, if at all, and certainly not in daylight.

In order to reach the fishing grounds of the upper river, we first have to go a long distance on a small tributary, winding our way carefully through a tunnel of mangrove trees with thick, strong roots and trunks larger than a man's body. They are the biggest mangroves I have ever seen, and they almost block out the sun. The boat moves smoothly through the morning water, and you can smell the foliage and the warm mud as you plow ever deeper into the mangroves. By 8:00 the insects—black flies, mosquitoes and others—are already on you.

After an hour of this, we hit the main river, turn south, and follow the river farther into the forest. When we reach the main river things begin to change. Colored birds and large parrots appear, their wings glinting in the light. The parrots mostly sit in the cradle of trees overhead, while smaller birds soar through the air, turning and gliding as if on a trapeze.

Strange, flowering plants border the river and old trees rise up from the green pools like the ghosts of ancient animals; their limbs and faces are slick and wet with moss and rain water. Some of them look dead but most are still alive, rooted in the muddy river bottom. There are big tarpon around their roots, down in ten feet of dark water, and as we start casting to them we begin to hear a hollow, drum-like sound. The sound grows louder as we cast into a landscape of red mahogany, serpentine green vines and extraordinry plants crawling down the bank—orchids I believe, but I'm not sure.

After a while we make a hard turn to the left, and there in the tangled silhouettes of the treetops we see the source of the noise: A gang of howler monkeys, shouting and screaming at us, showing their teeth and almost foaming at the mouth. The roar becomes nearly deafening as we slip past them on a green ribbon of water. It is indeed beautiful.

"What kind of trees are those?" I asked the guide.

He told me the name, which I can't now remember, then added something that raised the hair on my neck: "The ancient people used them to make canoes," he said.

"Who?"

"I just told you. The ancient people."

"Who were they?"

"I'm not sure, exactly. They have different names. It all depends on who you talk to."

"And the ruins of Altun Ha?"

"They made those, too."

"How do you know that?"

"Everybody knows that. But there are some people who still live here, back in the jungle, who know more than I do about those things—the medicine of trees and plants, the big cats, the jaguars, and many other things about the ancient people, even what the stones say at Altun Ha."

As he spoke I looked upstream and saw two men with skin like ebony. Their carved wooden canoe was anchored at the water's edge and they were busy mending an old net while keeping an eye on a fishing line hanging over the side of the canoe. The line was in a deep groove in the gunwale, worn there by time and heavy use. I could only imagine how many tarpon and snook had been wrestled into the bottom of that canoe over the years.

Without thinking, I waved to them and I wondered if they had caught anything. Their teeth flashed as they both smiled and waved back. Then one laughed, turned excitedly to the other and handed him a small coil of line; in the exchange I saw something—a boat filled with dancing phantoms, black-skinned and still beautifully alive, floating on a green river, and I marveled at the way the tendons and muscles in their arms drew tight as they knotted the line and then flung it down into their own reflections.

At that moment I guess some of it came to me: What I love most about all this isn't really the fish I catch or don't catch; it's the joy of being turned inside out in a place that is still connected to the earth as it has always been—and suddenly I am there, too, back where it all started, at the root of things, alive and free and perfect. Who wouldn't love that? It's a grand feeling.

After that I went to Mexico in May but not much happened except I had a couple of really good fishing days. There were some tuna around and we had fun with them for a while. I fished with a cab driver and writer from San Francisco, a man named Mike Rosa, and we had a good time with a small kind of tuna called a "skipjack." Mike didn't care much for anything too fancy, so we got along fine. We drank a lot of beer and talked about everything from some of the girls we knew a long time ago to music and anything else that came to mind.

Another guy, John Rysanich, who is one hell of a fly tyer, fished with us, and one day it was so good the three of us forgot about everything else. The only real thing was that we were hauling in one tuna after another in a small white boat with the blue Sea of Cortez heaving under the deck and our bare feet.

In late June I went back to Belize and fished with a guide named "Pops." His real name is Winston Cabral and he's famous as a bonefish guide. He loves tarpon, too, and we ignored everything else and tried for them all week, but I never hooked one. Nothing. A friend got one, a small fish (for a tarpon) of about twenty pounds, on one of my fly patterns and we both liked that. After five days of fishing I finally hooked a small bonefish on a shallow-water flat and Pops started laughing at me.

"Well, Waller, at least you aren't skunked now," he said.

Near the end of July I fished in Mexico again and we tried for marlin and sailfish, dragging a couple of big rubber lures behind the boat to attract the fish to the surface. The marlin or sailfish come up to see what's splashing and making all the noise and are fooled into thinking the lure is a fish to eat. When that happens you reel the lure closer and closer to the boat and hopefully they follow it. When they are near enough to reach with a short cast, maybe twenty feet, you jerk the lure away from them and your partner throws a fly right at them, or just to the side of them.

The first morning, when I least expected it, a large striped marlin came in hard from the left, on my lure, and it was my job to "tease" it close enough to the boat for my partner, Lou, to get a shot at it with a fly. The ocean just blew up with the fish, and I saw how big it was even as I looked down at my feet to make sure the deck was clear in case Lou got a cast. Marlin are not fish. When they swim, they seem more like prehistoric birds from an alien world. When they are excited, they light up in a shimmering, cellular brilliance, with their blue pectorals out stiff and erect, extended in oceanic flight, ancient, strong and beautifully alive, and they are powerful beyond anything I have ever had on a hook and line. The rod feels so small; when you cast to one, the whole affair seems almost futile—the act of a fisherman who will do anything to feel the kind of strength they have.

Somehow Lou landed that fish we hooked that first morning; two hours later I finally touched the leader in the middle of a summer storm, with the bright sun in half the sky and a pouring silver rain falling from the other. We were floating on the edge, going in and out of the sunshine and cooling rain as the fish drew the line tight and Lou fought it hard all the way as we watched. The ocean was as slick and smooth as a pearl, and alive with dimpling raindrops. I've never seen the sea like that before. It looked sweet beneath the shower, not like saltwater at all.

Neither Lou nor I will probably ever duplicate that fish, but we let it go. I watched it disappear like the great bird it was, growing smaller and smaller until even its blue wings and long copper bill were no longer there, and nothing else either, just the sound of our breathing and the rain falling on the ocean.

My steelhead fishing began in September as it always does, up in British Columbia, and this year I added a trip to Kodiak Island in Alaska. The big grizzlies are still there despite the hunting and poaching, and they shared the river with us while we fished for steelhead and they hunted for dying salmon in shallow pools along the ragged edges of mossy banks. We were camped on the river in their territory, and at night the thin nylon wall of the tent was the only thing separating them from me. I couldn't hear them at night, but I knew they were there just the same and they tore up another camp three nights in a row as we tried to sleep in ours.

Sorry for wandering around with all of this. I need to get on with the real reason for this letter and finish our brief telephone conversation of the other night. Scruffy died four days ago and I can't stop thinking about it.

I know fishermen are supposed to have dogs, but this cat was really different and more than I ever bargained for. He was certainly the equal of any dog I have ever seen or owned, including my Ridgeback, who I took to Montana with me, if you remember, and your own Ursa.

I never took Scruffy fishing but I always wanted to. He would have been great. He had it in him.

It's been twelve years since Judy found him in a cardboard box in the parking lot of a supermarket, on a Sunday when I wasn't paying any attention to much of anything except myself, probably dreaming about my next fishing trip. She brought him to the car and introduced me to him, and he laid in her hand like a flying squirrel, his tiny feet going out in all directions and his big green eyes telling me that if I messed with him even once I would pay dearly for it. Yet as Judy held him, he purred and I couldn't help but notice he was licking her fingers. She had been looking for a kitten, and for months had held steadfastly to the idea that the right one would in fact find her, and all she had to do was remain open to the possibility. I found the notion naive. How can cats find people?

"Well, he's cute enough," I said. "Maybe we should take him home."

His head was too big for his body and his ears stuck out like two furry triangles. His feet were as white as milk and they looked like snowshoes. When we got him home he was too small to climb the stairs but tried anyway, growling and gritting his teeth as he hung suspended from each carpeted riser, digging in like a mountaineer and slowly pulling himself up to the next step until at last he reached the top of the stairs and found his way to my fishing room and office. Sometimes it would take him a full half hour to do it and I couldn't stand to watch. I always helped him.

About a month and a half after he came home with us the terrier next door decided to dig a hole under the fence and come into our back yard and have at him, one bite at a time. This dog hated cats and would try to kill one if he found it in a defenseless position. The terrier's owner did nothing about it and in fact bragged about his dog over the telephone one day as he sat in the patio on the other side of the fence, drinking beer and listening to something he evidently believed was music. I happened to be in the yard when his dog finally broke through, and I swear I'm telling you the truth when I say the terrier was four times as large as the cat my wife loved with all her heart and which was even beginning to capture my attention.

Scruffy was in his usual place on our patio, sleeping quietly in a Mexican pot I had lined with an old blanket. He was not yet fully grown and the terrier hit Scruffy like a bomb, smashing the pot like a kamikaze straight from hell, but there was nothing I could do. I remember thinking the damn dog would kill the kitten that had no idea what had just attacked it, or why.

I needn't have worried; the shitty little terrier simply disappeared in a tornado of flying fur, razor-sharp claws, broken pieces of red pottery, and a blur of fighting fury that scared the hell out of me and sounded like the end of the world. And I'll always believe that's what the dog thought it was.

The terrier spun around in retreat as the bravest cat I ever knew hung onto his flanks, drove him back under the fence and into the yard of a neighbor I didn't like to begin with. That night, for the first time, Scruffy slept next to us on the bed, with some of my best fly-tying feathers tied together in a fake sparrow I made for him.

That was the beginning of the end for me. I was falling in love with a cat.

And there was more. Each time I'd pack for a trip—and I mean every time, for twelve years, without regard for time of night or day—Scruffy would be there with me, watching me sort out rods, clothing and his favorite things, my fishing reels. He loved the reels most of all and would come running when he heard the screech and click of their gears as I checked each one, for he knew I would let him have the end of the fly line to play with as I continued my preparations.

Sometimes I'd hit the lawn for casting practice and he'd come running when he heard me stripping line from the reel. I'd attach a piece of yarn to a shooting head and fish for him, throwing the yarn as far as I could with a big steelhead rod while Scruffy flew after it. He liked the yarn, but his favorite toy was a small stuffed rainbow trout. Judy and I had tried all kinds of things but all were of only temporary interest to him. Only the toy trout consistently held his interest—a great source of pride, for nothing more or less than an aging fisherman full of sentimentality. I knew he was getting sick when he stopped curling up around the trout.

Scruffy the Cat

When I called home from British Columbia this past week, it was during the best steelhead run in fifty-two seasons, or so people said. But when I heard about Scruffy and the fight he was in, I couldn't fish anymore. The river was out of me, and none of it seemed worth a damn. Not compared to that cat. I returned home the next day and walked into the bedroom and saw something I will never forget.

It was his last battle and he was losing badly. He looked at me as soon as I entered the room and meowed softly through the heat of his abdominal cancer. I stood there not knowing what in hell I could or should do.

The light was low in the room, the windows drawn, almost dark. Scruffy was sitting on his corner of our bed like a sphinx, with his haunches coiled and ready, but his strength was obviously gone. Yet his eyes were still beautiful—perfectly round and almost Egyptian, with dilated pupils as black as onyx floating in an ocean of incandescent gold. His eyes filled the room, the last refuge of his power and personality.

I knew then that the beautiful smoke of his life was almost gone. I lay down next to him and looked at him for what seemed like a very long time. There's no way I can prove this, but I know he was considering me and who, or what, I might really be. Beyond this I don't know what he was thinking, but I hoped he knew that I loved him. The next morning we surrendered him to the arms of a surgical nurse and Judy and I watched through a wire-screened window as the nurse placed him on a cold steel table in an unfamiliar room. He never complained; he simply turned and looked at us one last time, huddled under the glare of fluorescent lamps suspended over checkered ceramic tile. He died that night, and when the call came from the hospital I almost lost it.

I put some things together for his cremation—a leather-bound sheepskin fly wallet that he loved to sit on, some flies he played with, one of my shoelaces he always liked to bat around as he sat at my feet while I dressed for work, and a poem I wrote for him. There was also a picture of Judy and me in bed with him. I didn't know what else to do.

This morning, as I drove to my office, I changed lanes just before the overpass north of Sausalito, the one over Richardson Bay, and my exit into town. I always wanted to fish for striped bass there, but I never got around to it. There was no wind today, not even a soft breeze, just one of those warm and beautiful November days when the water is like glass, giving up a perfect reflection in which every detail is inverted, yet cleanly focused.

As I moved into the outside lane I could see all the concrete buildings and whitewashed homes with their magazine lawns and white picket fences reflected in the water, turned upside down in the mirror. The trees were growing down into the sky below although they moved in the wind as I drove over them. To my right, an old wooden bridge arched over a small creek that trickles into the shallow end of the bay during low tide. It was like a painting.

But there was something missing from the image, so I made up the rest. A fisherman sat at the water's edge, and a large, ring-tailed cat with white feet next to him, both looking down into the water. The fisherman's line was out but there was nothing on the end of it because there aren't any steelhead or salmon in the creek any more and even the bass don't run past the bridge like they once did. But it would be obvious to anyone who looked that the fisherman and the cat were having one hell of a good time.

See you soon,

Lani

Playing the Numbers

Most of the steelhead come in September and early October, congregating along miles of wilderness pools beneath a palette of unforgettable autumn colors. They are not ordinary steelhead; many are giants, weighing more than thirty pounds. In my opinion, although I've never caught one, some may exceed forty pounds. At least I've never caught one yet.

Any of them may rise to a surface fly on any pool at any time. Some come quickly and purposefully while others rise delicately, showing only a silver slip of water as the fly disappears in a tiny whirl-pool the size of a thimble. Those not disposed to rise often willingly take a submerged pattern with a strong, short pull that can break a fifteen-pound tippet and your heart at the same time. I've cut my hands from the tension of the line, bruised and torn my fingers on the spinning handle of the reel and watched in disbelief as a great fish cleared the surface and then fell like thunder into a pool so still and soft the contrast seemed impossible.

Everything seems to freeze when that happens, and the image remains on the lenses of your eyes like a dream in slow motion—a twisting, spiraling, soaring, silver-and-red trout suspended in the air. Then suddenly it is all over and your hands are shaking. At times, especially in September when the air is beautifully cold, the water still warm and the steelhead at their peak, the act of fishing for these steelhead seems like the flagging of a passing train.

Today is September 17, 1998. I am writing this as I look past two frosted panes of glass that fit snugly into the carefully mitered wooden frame of my cabin window. The cabin is about three dozen miles downstream from the lake where all this begins. The river is strong here, stronger than above, having gained volume from several tributaries, including the glacial Nilkitkwa and Shelagyote, and now, in the late afternoon light, I can see the water slipping easily past me, gliding through a magnificently steep mountain corridor and through a yellow arch of autumn cottonwood and aspen. The leaves flutter like tambourines, my favorite way of seeing and hearing them. In the morning, mist will leave the river as the sun comes streaming over the tops of a forest that has never been cut.

The fishing has been nothing short of incredible. The adjectives circulate around camp until they seem almost cheap, overused in our haste to voice words and numbers as we tumble out of boats and head for a hot shower and some whiskey at day's end. Fishing like this may never happen again. From my windowed perspective it seems appropriate simply to stop for a while, let some of it sink in, and make a few notes before getting on with preparations for the next day's fishing. The second scotch is in front of me—no ice, just large, warm and smooth. It goes down like silk. Easy.

Next to the amber glass sits my reel with its sink-tip line frayed from scraping over rocks. The line also is cracked from too many casts, and near the point where the sinking tip joins the running line is a bump—a "wind" knot that has become welded into the line, by a bad forward cast, defying all efforts at removal. I put it there late in the day on the last shimmering pool, a place called "Blue Flag," when I punched the rod too hard and too soon, trying for another yard or so of distance out to where I thought a steelhead might be lying.

No, that's not quite it—I knew exactly where they were, or at least where they should have been. The steelhead in the center of Blue Flag are like thoroughbred horses, heavily muscled, and nervous at the starting gate, just to the side of the roar and tumble of the rapids and downstream from the rock that resembles an elephant.

As my line drifts toward them I can almost feel their desire to rush forward and inhale the fly, a self-centered anthropomorphic fantasy at best. When the pull comes it's usually in a certain part of the pool, just as the floating, visible tail of the line moves out of the watery orange triangle formed by the reflection of a cottonwood painted in autumn colors.

Two were there today—a fat buck with a strong throat and funny-looking mouth, a real porker as they say, and the Queen of Diamonds that took the first cast after lunch. Five seconds later she was into the backing. Again and again I saw her flash in the sun, jumping as if her life depended on it, hanging in the air like a silver crescent moon against a sky of trees so purple in the shade they hovered on the edge of darkness. She was, as they say, beautiful and I loved her.

When she came ashore, rolling over on her jeweled sides, my hands were trembling and my breath was a cloud of vapor. I was on my knees for her in that moment of truth which always freezes me, and has for forty years, and she was indeed something to behold, even with the spot of blood where the fly had pierced her mouth. She looked at me and I wondered how she perceived what she saw. She was larger than I'd thought—maybe eighteen pounds or better—perfectly formed, as smooth and sleek as a pearl.

I always wonder: Why do I have to beat them at this game I make up and love so much, and when I have done so, and have them down in the cold gravel, why does it feel the way it does? As my wife says, "It's all very well, dear, but why do you have to bother them? They aren't hurting anyone." I think of the fringe groups out there that would ban such sport and me with it; looking over my shoulder, I see no trace of demonstrators in the woods, no signs being waved by young idealists with cherubic eyes, puckered mouths and wagging fingers. No periscopes appear in the center of the pool; even Cousteau's sub isn't here yet.

I go back to the fish's eye—crystalline, haloed yellow with an onyx center, black and unblinking. Staring at me. I am now her savior, her personal surgeon. The hook is removed, as gently as possible, and along with it any traceable responsibility. The lunatic fringe of Greenpeace will never find me out.

That's because, I tell myself, everything is really in reverse here. I am the one who has been captured, not the fish. I am in truth, a captive of the almost inescapable prison of ordinary routine, and I want out now and then from the "civilized" layers of urban concrete, asphalt and plastic that seem endless. I think of the man in front of me on the daily commute: I remember his burning eyes and armor-plated face while he leaned on the horn, shouting and screaming obscenities as he bullied his way in and out of smoky traffic, trying to push everyone out of his way. He was going much too slow to suit him, a beetle crawling slowly up the San Pedro grade between Novato and San Rafael. A man in trouble.

Finally, on the downgrade just west of Corte Madera and under a rising sun, he got to open it up, burning it hard, and sped away swiftly, to spend, I suppose, the day at a desk in some air-conditioned office under a fluorescent light that looked like ice, surrounded by dusty plastic ferns with no real air anywhere. My own predicament was not the same but seemed no less urgent; perhaps more so. Without complaining I remained quietly in my lane in the long string of metallic insects. I braked and accelerated dutifully, the obedient larva.

But now, here, I am outside, where I have just subdued this best of all trouts, after she went flying in the sun, jumping and sailing through an atmosphere it is still possible to inhale without changing the color of your lungs. I look at her again. She is powerful, with no faults or mistakes, beautiful and uncomplicated.

And then I look at myself, and realize the answer to my wife's patient, well-intentioned question—why do you bother them?—is intensely personal. The truth is I want to catch as many as I can, but only on my terms, which always seem to change: this season my terms include swimming flies with long curling wings and soft shoulders of red, lavender and cobalt, flies fashioned from feathers of the macaw, ibis, blue heron or other stately birds, from materials with colors and textures so sensual they remind me of exotic women in lace and flaming dress.

I can see all these and more when the fly is delivered on a long filament of line that uncurls in the warm sunlight. At times it seems as if I am pushing and pulling the whole world on a long string as I drive the fly into a beautifully clouded sky, gripping the long rod that lets in all the electrical juice—wired to the universe.

In truth I not only want to catch as many as I can, I want the largest, too—but I don't know how many I must have, how many must yield before I am off the hook and cross, transformed, stronger than before, snapped back into place, unzipped, warm and no longer crawling over rocks? How many before I am out of the routine and far away from the possibility that I may, in the end, be just like everyone else trapped on the freeways and concrete centers of ordinary American culture? I don't know the number.

In any event, the fish in front of me is more honest than I will ever be, and carries little more than the desire to return to her river and spawn. In her body, as I touch it, are at least the elementary beginnings of her eggs—two soft female envelopes called skeins, long strands of clustered opal, one on each side just below her spine, back a little from her heart, deep in her belly. Soft and ripening, some 1,500 of them remain in the darkness inside her, waiting for at least this part of her journey to end, and theirs to begin. Of these, only five to ten eventually will make it back themselves—past the predators, the disease, the winter floods, the searing rake of gill nets and hammered silver spoons, even the rather stupid-looking Egg-Sucking Leeches, and God knows what else.

There's another reason why I do this, and I don't know how you slice it any better than this: Like her counterparts, this solitary steelhead remains one of the most beautiful expressions of life I will ever encounter.

Back behind the cabin window, I think maybe my line is all right and I'll just leave it on the reel because I can't get the knot loose. Anyway, it's the last line I have of this type. If I draw Blue Flag again tomorrow I'll use another line, a thirty-foot shooting head backed by monofilament, an easy formula for reaching the ninety-plus feet you must be able to cast in Blue Flag. The guides, Mark and Billy, always say the same thing when you get out of the boat: "This is a caster's pool. Wade deep, as deep as you can, shoot the hell out of the line and make damn sure you swing it through the seam out there." It must be in the guide's manual, or maybe they just made it up.

The seam "out there" is at least ninety feet away and to do the job properly the fly and leader should crack the 100-foot mark. Otherwise you get a drift the size of a pencil and, as a friend once advised, "The fly is out of it before it ever gets in it."

"Go to hell," I tell the guides. "You know I can't do it."

One good thing: In most places Blue Flag requires no mending. The monofilament merely tags along, itself obedient and perfect, just behind the slowly drifting line. The hardest part is stuffing seventy feet of shooting line in your mouth.

I suppose I could learn to use a two-handed rod, at least here, but it seems I'm too stubborn, or maybe just too old now to really give a damn. I'm having too much fun. Maybe later. Maybe next year.

Consider this: two boats with eight anglers out of Silver Hilton, the camp where I am staying, have just accounted for eighty-one steelhead to the fly.

In one day.

Of these, five were twenty pounds or better. Three were more than twenty-five. One, a thick-bodied brute taped out at forty-two inches with a twenty-four-inch girth. It had shoulders like a horse and blood-colored flanks as thick as those belonging to one of the river's Chinook salmon, now long spawned out and gone for sure. Steelheading. Just another word for madness.

Darkness. I've mended the line as well as I can. Billy Labonte, one of the guides, comes to the cabin looking for me. His eyes are as white as porcelain saucers with bright blue centers and he waves his arms like an osprey trying to gain altitude. I think of him as a son, in a way, and I guess that's why I've tried to spoil him. That, plus the certain knowledge that I need him. My legs are finally beginning to go. I'll be needing a lower gunwale in a few more seasons when I try to jump in the boat after wrestling waist deep with Blue Flag for two hours and I want him ready to help.

"It was amazing," he says. "They were everywhere! We hooked forty-one."

Mark Macaneely, the other guide, was just as happy, but sanity eventually prevailed as he and Billy shared stories. After all, the four anglers in Mark's boat hooked only thirty-eight.

Mark, now in his fourth season, is as sharp as a knife, but soft-spoken and quietly sure of himself. On his first day of guiding he came downriver as I stood like a zombie on the stiletto edge of a shale precipice, unable to go any farther and with ten feet of dark, roaring water just inches from my toes. He drove the boat right over my backing, which was stretched tight as a bowstring, disappearing into the fog down river. Jesus. The boat cut through the lemon-colored Dacron and severed its connection with a huge, burning steelhead in a smooth pool called "Pig Pen." The only one I hooked that day.

It didn't matter. If you wait long enough, what goes around comes around. Earlier this week it all came back with interest. Mark put me in The Pen, smiled as he left with the thumbs-up thing he does, and on four consecutive casts I rolled four fish, one well above twenty pounds, a large male that broached the surface like a dark seal. I landed that and a smaller one with a wound on its shoulder, probably eighteen pounds and very tired. I never saw the others. One broke the fifteen-pound test leader on the first pull. Maybe someday I'll learn to drift the fly with the heel of my right hand off the rim of the reel. The other escaped for reasons unknown.

This evening I am glad for Mark and Billy, for myself, and for the other anglers who have come here hoping for just such a thing. What a day. The week has been even better: 457 steelhead hooked. On flies!

The two lodges upriver report similar phenomena: Pierce Clegg's Norlakes Lodge is cracking them hard and Chick Stuart's Babine River Lodge says the same. The word hisses and sparks through the radio static and everyone knows it's true, with no need for distortion or competitive exaggeration. Not this season. This is the year of all years, the ultimate, the best in more than a half century, they say.

Numbers. Always numbers. I try not to get too involved with them, although I find them hopelessly attractive at times. They are only the most basic of descriptions, and for me they can sometimes go too far: If you catch too many, and I have at times, and if you aren't careful, and I haven't been at times, something is lost and sooner or later you're all alone with something everyone looks at, but no one likes to see.

A case in point: Not too long ago I watched a fisherman—an elderly gentleman, or so it appeared—hook a fish in a pool called "The Patch" on a nearby river. As he fought the fish, he began giving a blow-by-blow description of the day's piscatorial events, an odyssey in which he had triumphed over many steelhead, proudly announcing to the rest of the assembled anglers—all five of us—that this was his "tenth steelhead of the day, goddam sonofabitch." On the same fly. On the same leader, and he hadn't even changed the tippet, as his new rod was a marvel of sensitivity with a butt to match. I'll say.

The fisherman was as large as a tree and he cursed the struggling fish as it came ashore, a rather odd response, I thought. He wore a long coat, too long really, which flapped around his waist in a wet snarl from crossing the river at a place no one thought possible.

"I had to cross," he said. "Sonofabitch. Number seven it was, or was it my sixth? Must have been thirty-nine-by-twenty-one. Oh my God, look at this bastard here jump, will you?"

A few moments later, when number ten was finished, the fisherman hovered over its silver body in the arrogant posture of an aging matador. Still cursing for no apparent reason and waving his rod in the air, he began kicking the fish in a panic-stricken way. "Number ten," he said once more, booting her around in the mud and silt until she pointed in the appropriate direction—apparently anywhere away from him, as if she might in gratitude and passion want to swim up his pants and service him—until finally she found her way back to the cooling, life-giving currents and disappeared. The fisherman could not even tell me what sex she was. That's because he hadn't even see her. I don't think he'd ever really seen a steelhead.

"Too many rivers," I thought, "or not enough."

Numbers. I remember now that the most steelhead hooked in one week here at Silver Hilton by one angler was 101. Mostly on lures. In six days. Four more days produced forty-three more to the same angler, a skilled companion with whom I have been fishing for more than twenty years.

"That's 14.4 per day," Carl says, and it was true. I was there. But I saw the look in his eyes when he described that trip and how he wanted still more, and I remember the day years later when he finally gave up lures and picked up a fly rod. He fished hard all day with the certain knowledge that if he had the hardware on, he might have a number of fish sufficient to get the monkey off his back.

"How many today?" I asked as he pulled off his waders in the cabin.

"One, but I got it at Floyd's on a dry fly and it ran like hell for 120, maybe more, on ten-pound test tippet and a No. 2 fly. Shit, it was fantastic! You should have seen it. I landed it on the bar just around the corner in three inches of water and it fought for forty-one minutes and I almost died it was so incredible."

"Catch your breath. More scotch?"

"Huh?"

On the other hand, if you aren't catching enough, it always seems to mean one thing: you're catching less than anyone else. That's happened to me at times, and I don't know which is worse, catching more or less than anyone else. And in the end, I've never decided what the right number is unless it could be the same for all of us, probably somewhere between six and 136 fish a day, all season long, year after year, until we all finally lost count and it didn't matter any more.

Numbers. Always numbers. There are two anglers on the gravel, just out of the boats, and the process begins. The conversation is polite, yet guarded. The chess pieces move carefully in their eyes as each tries to ease his curiosity about the other. They've been doing this for a long time.

"Howdy."

"Hullo."

"Good day?"

"Yup."

"How many?"

"Four. You?"

"Same."

It's getting interesting, a possible tie, and one thinks about his equipment as he looks at the other's. They come closer to one another, knowing the moment of truth is fast approaching. Each smells potential victory.

"Any size to 'em?"

"Thirty-nine by twenty and a half, and thirty-six and a quarter by seventeen, and thirty-four by sixteen and three quarters, and thirty-five and three quarters by seventeen and a quarter. On a nine-weight rod, twelve-pound test and a No. 1/0 Pink Marauder. You?"

"Thirty-seven and a half by seventeen and a quarter, and thirty-six and three quarters by eighteen and a half, and thirty-five and a quarter by sixteen and five-eighths, and thirty-six and a half by eighteen and a half. A No. 2 Black Mamba, No. 10 rod and 15-pound test."

"Say, I hear the stock market crashed today and there's a serial killer loose in California."

"How bad was the market?"

"Dunno. Really bad. People are jumping out of the windows. Heard it on the radio."

"Hmmm . . . Hey, how big was your biggest again?"

"Forty by twenty-one."

Now it's really getting dark. The third and final scotch, smaller this time. Dinner is long gone. Everyone else has been asleep for hours. The snoring is getting louder as my bunkmates get deeper into it. I think it's raining, but I don't know. At least the lemming hasn't found its way back under my covers. Last night, while I tried to sleep, the little bastard ran up my bare leg with feet that scratched—moving, nocturnal midnight fur with teeth like serrated chisels. I wonder what they eat. Meat? If it ever does that again, it'll get a chiropractic adjustment it won't forget.

I close my eyes and meet myself on the river. I've done it. Two of them. "Forty-three by twenty-six, eh? Thirty-nine and a half pounds, eh? On a dry fly. Congratulations," I say, shaking my own hand. The dialogue continues: "What time is it?"

It's 3:00 in the morning and you can't sleep. Is it raining?"

"I said, I don't know."

"Shut up and go to sleep."

"I can't."

"Well, think about something else. Think about. . . ."

"I tried that. It didn't work."

"Oh hell. I'm getting back up."

"Whaat!?"

"I'm changing the cracked line."

"Not that again."

Some unmeasurable time later and half asleep at last, I look out into the darkness and something is on the front porch—the elephant rock at the throat of Blue Flag has come alive, clomping around on the front porch of the cabin, ivory-white tusks shining in the moonlight. It comes to the window and peers in at me with two very large, bright yellow eyes. Then the elephant blinks and I see the crusty folds of its eyelids drop down like a wrinkled leather curtain, then go up again as he comes closer and breathes frost on the glass. Shit! He sees me. I stop my own breathing and don't make a sound. His tusks are pressed against the window now. What if he comes through the wall?

Something snarls. Maybe it's Carl or Jack, both of whom snore, or worse, all night long. Or maybe it's a leopard on the roof, and it's not really rain I hear pattering up there. Who knows? Anything can happen. This is fishing, isn't it?

In the blue vapor of early dawn just across the river, General George Armstrong Custer and his men are setting up camp in dirty woolen coats. How did they get into this? I can smell their campfires, but the horses are nervous and the men are not going anywhere and I turn back to the elephant. There is something on top of him, but I can't quite . . . Wait a minute . . . Jeez, this is too much. It's a friend, rod builder Jerry Kustich of Winston Rod, just back from the Gulf of Tonkin with another load of Chinese cane.

"Not enough lasagna last night," says an internal voice, "and too much scotch. Or is it the other way around?"

"I don't know," a second voice responds. "Maybe you need medication. But I don't think so, just a little more sleep would be fine, nurse. Thank you."

Jerry, who is no slouch as an angler, ignores me and is now doing tricks with the elephant as I try to wake up. He is hanging on as the animal stands on two huge legs, shaking its head and thundering up and down on the porch, waving its trunk and rear end around in the air. Kustich is dangling an assemblage of things in front of the elephant's trunk—Swiss chard, watermelon rinds, a bag of peanuts, and an endorsement contract with Winston Rod Company—all served up on an eight and a half-foot, two-piece quadrate rod and a nine and a half-foot leader with a twelve-inch 100-pound shock tippet and sixteen-inch class section of twenty-pound test, the latter the maximum allowed by the International Game Fish Association. He'll need it if the animal takes. The elephant's ears are tremendously large and ragged, an old veteran no doubt. Jerry tips his ringleader hat and, as the brass and percussion sections inside the cabin really open up, he winks at me, pulling on a red silk banner that unrolls down the side of the elephant. "Bamboo Lives!" it proclaims.

The elephant sees the bait as it swings by the third time. He has it. Jerry sets the non-existent hook and the elephant lurches forward. The quadrate stretches and curves dangerously as the elephant turns its gigantic head as if to locate the origin of its discomfort. Suddenly he understands and turns away, lumbering quickly off the porch and into the foggy night. Kustich is fighting like hell and the little cane rod is jumping. I can almost hear the splinters.

"For God's sake, Jerry!" I shout, "Give him some line. He'll break the damn rod."

The midnight pachyderm runs away, its massive buttocks swaying. He's going to take Jerry across the river! The elephant is already in midstream, but Kustich is still with him. The pachyderm looks even larger now and so strong, clearly the largest I have ever seen. He plants each foot slowly and carefully in the rapids, crushing small rocks and dislodging larger ones as he holds steady in the current, still shaking his head and trying to free himself from the steady pull as Jerry shouts and the sun rises. The tippet is now grinding against one of the tusks.

For a long time, the elephant holds firmly in the current using its body to maintain position as Jerry pours it to him. Then he begins to move again. Carefully estimating the distance to shore and flagging his ears like sails, he plods on. I think he's getting tired.

He emerges on the far side of the river, and I watch the Babine drop eight inches as the elephant steps to shore swaying weakly from side to side, and what do you know? He collapses. It's almost over now, as Jerry kneels over him, grinning, trying to hold his catch by the tail with one hand while he puts his other under its stomach so I can get the photo. This could be a brochure shot.

Suddenly the elephant regains its strength, lurching free. Then he and Jerry begin to blur in the brightening sunlight.

"How big was it"? I ask.

"Really big," Custer answers excitedly, going for his sword, but it's too late.

As the sun emerges, Kustich and his trophy disappear into the lush foliage on the far side of the river. Shit. I've lost the endorsement contract and the photo. Just before they fade, I am saved from a future of eternal guesswork about the size of the elephant, because I see something: a tattoo on his gigantic hindquarters. Jerry turns for one last look at me and is smiling. His face is an emerging sun of blinding light. He knows.

Of course. I was right. This is no ordinary elephant. No sir. This is the biggest elephant I have ever seen. I look again and there it is, in plain sight. The inscription on his butt reads: "1,954 by 772 1/2." Multiply those two numbers, square them and then divide by 800, add two pounds for a Babine male, and you know what you get? I'll tell you what you get. A new world record! That's what you get.

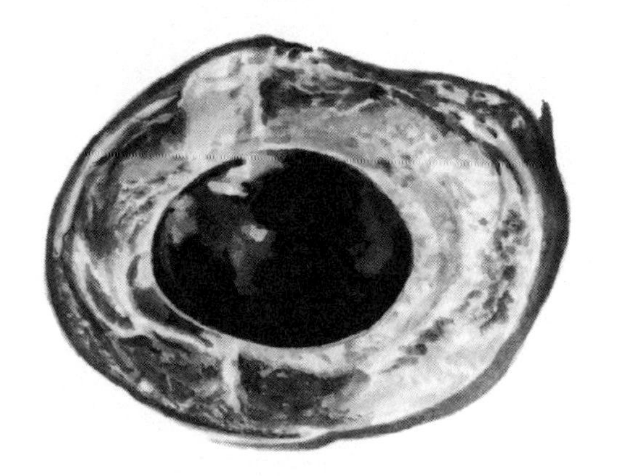

Eye of the Marlin

Most of Ixtapa and Zihuantenejo are asleep in a dark heat. The temperature is eighty degrees. It's late April, fishing season, and three American anglers will go out today on an early charter.

Standing together in the murky light of their hotel lobby, the three get their lunches from a sleepy concierge and introduce themselves to one another. The young married couple is from Iowa. The third person is a solitary American angler who is celebrating his birthday. All three speak in morning language, soft and polite, especially the woman, who smiles and clutches a red purse, a small picnic basket and a book. She usually does not do this kind of thing and appears somewhat nervous.

Her husband usually doesn't do this kind of thing either and he says little during the ten-minute cab ride drive from the hotel in Ixtapa to the wooden dock that is home to the small fishing fleet of Zihuantenejo. Today they will fish for marlin aboard the thirty-two-foot glass-and-mahogany cruiser *El Presidente.*

White and angular, the outriggers of the boat form a large V, and to the fishermen it resembles a floating bird; even at the dock the outriggers appear as outstretched wings. Steaming coffee is passed to the three Americans as the boat's diesel grudgingly chugs to a start. Lines are gathered and *El Presidente* is suddenly loose in a swirl of choking blue smoke.

"Senors, we must first get bait," the captain announces as the steady clack of the diesel pushes the boat past the bay of Zihuantenejo toward the open ocean. The solitary angler looks down into the water; the wake is a trailing river of foam and bubbles barely visible in the dawn. It looks like a galaxy of stars, some as silver as ice, others strange shades of blue or emerald, all strung out on the dark water as the boat moves onward and the adobe shadows of Zihuantenejo grow smaller.

Only the young deckhand seems alive and animated; he scurries around like an insect, checking drag settings on the reels, polishing their side plates, swabbing the deck, climbing up to the captain's chair, then down again in the semi-darkness.

Once past the bay two small rods appear; the two anglers each take one from the deckhand, who ignores the woman. She remains polite and nervous, but interested, and she withdraws carefully to the cabin with another cup of coffee, watching closely, holding her book as the port rod is rigged with a pink lure, a tiny rubber squid with glaring white eyes and curling tentacles that flare when the teardrop sinker goes home inside its head. The squid runs high, bobbing and weaving only a foot or so beneath the surface. Sometimes it comes to the top, gulps a splash of saltwater and air, then goes back down. The starboard rod has a tin bait. Heavy, triangular, and shiny, it drops quickly beneath the transom and the swirling trail of stars.

Dawn arrives. A rising sun illuminates the horizon in a blaze of light, changing each wave from black to pink to orange, then briefly to silver, finally to turquoise and white with the reflected image of the cruiser. Something crackles over the radio but is lost in static. Maybe another boat, maybe the mainland; who knows?

Suddenly the pink squid is sucked quietly from the surface. Then, almost simultaneously, a second fish flashes deep and takes the metal bait. Three minutes later two small bonito come easily to the transom, victims of the irreversible crank of identical reels and 80-pound test lines.

"Ahh! Bueno, bueno amigos," comes the shout from the bridge. The captain sets a southerly course, clips the wheel, and drops down on deck to introduce himself. He appears crisp, clean-shaven and immaculately dressed in a starched white shirt. He has long, wiry, muscular arms and strange eyes: small, brown, and nervous, they move like a sparrow in agitated flight, resting on nothing for long, certainly not the eyes of others. They flicker as he shouts instructions to the deckhand, who snatches the bonito from both lures. Lacing each bait expertly, finishing the truss and rigging them with 12/0 razor-sharp hooks, the young man transfers them to heavy lines rigged to heavy rods and reels, then clips them to the outriggers.

Resting in sockets above and behind the seated anglers, the rods point skyward, waiting. Each bonito is down and racing headlong through the water sixty-five feet behind the boat and thirty to forty feet below the surface. The polished reels shine like gold in the sun.

"Eighty-pound test!" the captain proclaims proudly. "Thees is my rods, my reels; and thees is my own boat," he says, opening his arms to embrace the boat and the entire circumference of the ocean in a single gesture, looking at no one in particular. The three guests acknowledge his proclamation, the couple almost deferentially, the solitary angler more directly.

"Captain," the solitary angler says, "if I get a marlin, I don't want to kill it. I want to release it. No muerto. Comprende?" He draws his index finger across his throat while shaking his head in the negative.

The angler wants a blue marlin badly. He wants it to be perfect and has dreamed of it since he was a boy. But he does not want to kill it.

"Oh, yah, si senor," the captain responds. "We don' wanna keel even one. Comprendo, comprendo." The two shake hands, striking a deal. Then the captain returns to the bridge.

For almost an hour nothing happens. The baits track behind the boat, hooked and in place. A pelican appears briefly, almost too far from land, looking for a handout. None is given. The white outrigger wings of the mahogany-and-glass bird still point upward toward a sky of gathering clouds. Maybe it will rain.

Now heading due east, *El Presidente* presses on, patiently cutting a triangular swath of electric blue water some ninety feet wide. Zihuantenejo is lost in umber haze and the sun is beginning to burn.

Another hour passes. Nothing.

Another thirty minutes. Still nothing.

Then it happens. From somewhere, perhaps to starboard and down under a spiral of descending yellow light, deep in cobalt a hundred feet below the surface, a great eye turns and sees the baits. Pectorals extend like blue wings, soaring through a sky of ocean. The bonito react to the oncoming threat. The water swirls invisibly as a black form streaks toward them and takes one, then the other. Both lines are ripped from the outriggers, snapping like two quick shots in the wind. Line peels. Ten yards, twenty, then forty, fifty, sixty until one hook suddenly pulls free. The other does not.

The drag lever of the lucky reel is pushed forward, engaged, clicking into place. In a split second the drag goes from zero to a howl and the hook goes in.

Holding the rod which has the marlin on, the captain is smiling. When he knows the fish has swallowed the bait, he shovels the tackle quickly to the starboard angler, choosing him for no apparent reason. The solitary angler takes it in his hands and rises to his feet, trying to see, but there is nothing on the surface. The line leaves the rod tip and disappears into oblivion. A hundred yards away and seventy-five feet below, the marlin turns briefly, and pauses, curious. Then it simply regurgitates the four-pound bonito and, trembling with strength, starts off again, well hooked, and ripping some 250 more yards of line. The white glass rod jumps uncontrollably down to the transom. The pressure is incredible.

"La cana! La cana!" the captain screams, motioning for the angler to sit in the chair and keep the rod butt off the transom board. He doesn't want it scratched.

Impossible. The marlin is now going down and away, deeper and deeper, past the columns of sunlight, deeper into turquoise, then down to indigo and beyond. All alone in 400 feet of water it pauses momentarily, then turns and heads due north. Another 150 yards of line disappear from the reel. The rod remains steady, pointing down toward the pull; the line strains. The angler braces himself. Nothing more can be done.

For the next half hour *El Presidente* obediently follows the fish, her five passengers watching silently, pulled through the ocean by a swimmer perfect in strength and form. Sweat stings the eyes of the angler who clutches the rod, his muscles cramping, dizzy and tired, fighting the urge to urinate, pumping and lifting, lifting and winding, pumping again. White moons of flesh appear and the blisters break open. He knows little about such tackle and is simply hanging on. The drag, set at an almost impossible ten pounds, is still slipping.

An hour later, at 10:00, the marlin still has not shown, but is closer. The line pierces the transom wake at an angle that keeps the rod tip almost doubled. The marlin's pull is steady, but the fish is nearer and circles back and forth, gliding beneath the foam, still tremendous and unyielding. The angler considers giving the rod to one of the other Americans. Maybe it would be better to give it to the woman. She hasn't taken her eyes off the angler or the tip of the rod for more than an hour. The thought is interrupted by the captain's frantic yell.

"La cana! La cana!" he screams once more, pointing as the rod dips again toward horizontal and beyond, resting temporarily on the transom.

"Goddammit, go to hell," the fisherman mutters to himself. "Screw la cana."

Now it is 11:30. The angler's arms, legs and back are almost gone, and even the thought of losing the fish no longer matters that much.

He was going to release it anyway. It has been almost five hours and everything can go to hell. Bracing his feet on the transom, he lifts, then lowers and turns the handle of the reel one more time. The line is singing, perhaps close to breaking as the deckhand crunches the drag past the point of no return. And then, finally, something new: Somewhere below, the dark form slowly begins to yield and lift, feeling softer. The rod is lowered again, line regained and the angler lifts again. The form yields once more.

An hour later, through a mist of pain, sweat and foul language, the angle of pull is at last shallow, the fish only a few yards away. Just beneath the transom a long form moves from right to left, then back again, then back once more, pacing like a tiger. Suddenly it turns, thick and broad, flashing in the sun, and the angler sees it for the first time. It is immense, still strong and bathed in luminescence as it emerges from the water, coming to the surface with its shoulders and back rolling, its dorsal stiff and erect, flecked with purple. The bill is extraordinary, like a black sword cutting through the water. And suddenly there it is: unexpected and almost unimaginable, 400 pounds of blue marlin swims in plain sight, just off the tip of the white rod, a living fire burning in the foam of a blue ocean two miles deep.

"Goddammit! Goddammit! Pull, senor, pull!" the captain screams above the diesel, the radio, and the roar of the fisherman's heart. The words are repeated and eventually reach the exhausted angler like a distant whisper. "Senor, you must pull. You must pull now!"

There is no pulling. There is no strength for it. Not any more. Looking curiously, unknowing, without malice, the marlin simply makes a single move with its tail and is at the transom, looking up, with the invisible pressure still in its mouth. And then the angler sees something he could not have imagined even as a boy: the living eye of a blue marlin weighing more than 400 pounds. The eye is circular and large, the pupil ebony, the iris a transparent silver halo of light. It is beautiful.

The gaffing is not seen. Only the first blow struck with a steel bar is noticed by the fisherman, and it comes as a sound struck just behind the marlin's bill and on the smooth slope of a beautifully carved forehead. Some of the cranium folds as the marlin responds and looks upward toward the unreasonable, mysterious pain.

"What could this be?" the fish seems to ask, looking at the five people and the boat it cannot understand. The answer comes as a second and third strike are delivered. The eye is frightened and flickers in the light, trying to get away. Blood vessels hemorrhage. The eyes of the captain are two black slits. He screams a Spanish oath to the deckhand, who obliges, taking an unused outfit and driving another hook into the smooth belly. He then hands it to the second angler who is standing all alone. "You pull now," the young mate commands.

The marlin's eye surveys each of the five humans in rapid succession, shifting from person to person, back and forth, beholding its tormentors as it is trussed, dragged to the transom, and beaten to death. Two ropes, a pair of gaffs, and two eighty-pound lines with 12/0 hooks now hang from its body and exquisitely sculpted head.

Now the marlin's eye is going. Transformed and lost in a blur of madness, it fades and begins to fill with blood, going from silver and onyx to pink with a red halo.

The angler who fought the marlin at last tries to interfere. "No, amigo. I said we would release it. Not this. We had a deal."

There is a pause. "Impossible, senor," the captain finally says. "He would have died. He was hooked too deeply. We could not save him. I had no choice."

He is lying. There is always a choice, no matter what the position of the hook. Marlin sells for ten American dollars a pound in Ixtapa. This one will bring almost $4,000.

The angler looks down at his hands. They are cut and trembling, the result of something never bargained for. Now what? He looks into the eyes of the captain who, for once, is staring at him, a greedy little bird of a man who knows the smell of money.

"There is no deal, senor." The captain squints the words.

The gulls seem to hear, and gather. Curious, hungry and staring as the marlin begins to die, they circle behind the transom as the angler fails his ideology and his fish. He says nothing, turns away from the captain and sits in the chair, barely three feet way from the dying animal. The marlin's eye is swallowing him. "You never told me," it says, "that it would be this way."

The dock at Zihunatenejo is alive with tourists, fishermen, small boys and barking dogs as *El Presidente* comes home to berth. The bay is muddy near shore, a blend of silt and turquoise stirring in the wind. It looks like green milk. The breeze is up now, as it usually is in the afternoon when the fishing boats return and flags are flying. *El Presidente* has only one, a marlin flag. Marlin Azul: Blue Marlin. The prize of prizes.

Gathering like a school of starving mullet, tourists collect as the fish is removed from the transom plate. Someone pops a flash camera and several others follow. Even the other captains are impressed. Words swirl around the wooden dock and through a Spanish breeze as the one with sparrow eyes gesticulates, waving his hands like a dancing moth, telling the story.

The marlin makes its final journey in the hot iron bed of an old truck. Grappled once more, for the last time, the fish is hoisted to the sky and hangs black in the sun like barbecued meat. Flies find it, like they always do, and drink corneal fluid from the rim of the marlin's eye as the angler looks on, sick of it all and alone with his thoughts, looking for some kind of redemption or escape, but there is none. Nothing.

He was taught better than this. Why did he fail? What happened? He looks past the staring tourists, the hanging corpse and the bay of green milk. He can see the dogs coming down from the hills and through the winding streets tonight. They, too, are licking the bony corpse, their teeth clicking under a lemon-colored moon. Inside the restaurant two sunburned tourists are drunk, and sit at the table drooling while they eat Marlin Azul. It is on the menu.

"Jesus Christ!" yells someone in the crowd. "Look at that. Who in hell caught it?"

The words reach the fisherman's ear and the truth is simple enough: He did, and for one moment of time, on a boat somewhere in Mexico, he lost himself and was not an angler or a man at all, not even a boy dreaming dreams. He was none of these. He was a coward.

"For Pete's sake," says a second voice, "doesn't anyone here know who caught this damn thing?"

I don't remember exactly what I said after that. Something rather silly and out of place, I'm sure. I do remember turning my back and pushing my way through the staring crowd as I walked to the cab waiting under a nearby tree.

That night I sat alone on the veranda of the hotel, looking down at the sea. It was indeed my birthday, my fifty-sixth. My wife, who had given the charter to me as a gift, knew something was wrong and remained silent inside our room, waiting for me to speak.

No sleep would come that night. The eye of the dead fish, its iris red like the sun, the pupil a black moon, circled the room hour after hour, looking down at me from a fantastic orbit of time which seemed impossible to measure. At one point, my wife, beautiful and near, seemed to know, even in her sleep. She reached out for me just before dawn, but a sudden breeze moved the curtains and I withdrew, moving across the room and over to the window to look once more at the ocean. I felt the burden of an indescribable weight, straining my muscles, shortening them, cramping them with pain. I was so tired. Where were my glasses? When I found them and put them on, my hands looked old and wrinkled in the dim light, the veins knotted, almost senile.

Another year had passed. How many more would there be? Would I ever see such a fish again? And if so, what would come of it?

I gathered the curtains, closing them, remembering my youth and how it was when I was a boy thinking about the fishing I would someday have, and the promises I had made to myself. In those days my tackle was simple—a few things my father had given me—and I loved it all. At the time, a fish such as the blue marlin was almost beyond my comprehension, and certainly beyond the circumstances of my life, but I always knew I would catch one someday, somehow, if I worked hard enough. When I visualized it, it always jumped like a bird, soaring, flying, shining in the sun, taking me to unknown and extraordinary places and feelings unreachable in any other way. And the fantasy always ended in the best way: after the battle, the fish would always turn to me, still suspended in the water, and when I looked in its eye a certain kind of loneliness I had would disappear.

Then the fish would go about its business, slipping away like a knife, diving effortlessly beneath the surface, free and gone forever, a departed brother. From this experience something was always added to the stock of my life, some kind of promise, some kind of guarantee. It is, I suppose, one of the reasons why some men like fishing so much, and why some of us will never get over it.

The Importance of Casting

The easiest deliveries are those made over small, shadowy trout in the thin water of high-mountain streams. Next easiest are streamer probes for rainbow and brown trout or the measured cadence of casts for steelhead in larger waters. The most difficult casts, the ones that will bring you to your knees, are on saltwater flats when you're running out of time, the wind is blowing and the target is swimming past you like a ghost. That is, if you can see the target at all.

For some people, the ability to cast perfectly comes very close to a moral necessity. Get this: according to calculations presented at one of the latest West Coast fishing trade shows, there are approximately twelve different casts that must be mastered before one can be considered an "expert." These include the roll cast, back cast, forward cast, single and double haul, Belgian and Steeple casts, the curve cast (including "positive" and "negative" curves) and the pile and dump casts. And when all these fail, there's always the change-of-direction cast.

You could add, the speaker said, the repertoire of the Spey-casting enthusiast: the single Spey, double Spey, Snap-T (also called "the chicks-dig-it cast") and the two-handed overhead cast.

And to further complicate the drama, single-handed casts could be done with two hands and double-handed deliveries could be achieved with one wrist and arm. Thus one could employ such beauties as the two-handed pile and dump cast and of course, the single-handed chicks-dig-it cast.

I listened to the guy and thought about what he said and decided I'd add a few others: The shovel cast, the ear lobe whiz and the buttocks stab.

When I was eleven years old and hard pressed for reasonable solutions to fishing problems beyond my ability to deal with at the time, I also considered the Winchester Model 94 Lever Action cast and once almost used it on a big brown that lived against an undercut bank. This was the last phase of a philosophical disintegration that began with a California Coachman fished both wet and dry on the same cast, followed by a souffle of cheese and finally a five-inch worm drifted past the lunker's root-wad cellar three days in a row. All to no avail. I could see his eye and never did get him. As someone once said, "Yessuh, that's right. If you can see them, they can see you. Yessuh."

In truth, I have made only three great casts in my life. The last was on a Canadian steelhead river and now, whenever I revisit the pool, I still don't know how in hell I did it. The pool is called "Spey," which is an appropriate name because there are trees right down to the shoreline on both sides of the river, leaving no room for a back cast. At the time I made the cast I wasn't using a Spey rod, however, and made the toss with a ten-foot single-handed rod.

On river right, the lie at Spey is a solitary boulder seventy feet away, in the middle of the river. You have to make the cast standing next to shore in water almost up to the top of your waders, with the riverside lodgepole and spruce nestled firmly against your butt; one would be better off fishing the pool from one of those casting platforms they have on some of the Scandinavian salmon rivers, or sitting in a float tube, or even standing on scaffolding attached to one of the trees, but Canadian regulations forbid all these. Probably a good thing, too; no sense adding those kinds of possibilities to the kind of gillnetting that goes on up there.

I actually made the cast twice, but I count it as only one cast because the efforts were exact duplicates. The first resulted in a little tick or bump on the line that I thought might be the boulder, but I wasn't sure. Next time, however, a fish took hold and eventually I beached a twenty-one-pound buck well below the lie in which I found him. As it turned out, he was snagged in the dorsal, but that seemed immaterial. I was so proud of the cast that everything else was academic and I never told the guide the fish was foul-hooked. Why bother? The guide was nineteen years old and at that age guides just don't understand. They don't understand because they have so much time left.

Over the years, my progress as a caster has been inspired by some who rank among the very best. One, West Coast casting guru Mel Krieger, confided to me many years ago that I could avoid casting a "closed" or "tailing" loop if I altered both my imagination and my casting and pretended I was throwing a tomato off the tip of the rod instead of beating wool from the hump of an innocent buffalo.

When I got into the business of fly fishing and travel in 1976, Lefty Kreh reminded me that I could always count on one thing: "The fly line always goes where the rod tip goes because the fly line isn't stupid." I never spent much time with Lefty after that, but I didn't need to. I found the comment sufficiently inspirational.

New Zealand guides understand the importance of casting and have helped much. At least two of them, Peter Church and Pete Flintoff, will have nothing to do with anything that even looks like a steelhead cast. "That's a goddamn Belgian cast, that's what it is," shouts Church, "and it's no good down here. Not accurate enough. Come over your shoulder in a straight line and forget about the rotation of your rod tip. One more of those and I'll gut you."

Flintoff is even less subtle. He tolerates some distance casting because he knows most anglers like the feel of the line's belly in the air to help them "load the rod," but if you don't throw most of your casts over the plate at forty feet you can see one eyebrow rise like a red-eyed moon above the smoking droop of his hand-rolled cigarette as he asks you when you had the sex-change operation.

I also thank the British Columbia guides and anglers who had to suffer through my temper tantrums and loss of faith as I took up casting the two-handed rod three years ago. For a while casting the "new" rods seemed roughly equivalent to standing naked on a California freeway during rush hour and flogging myself with a whip. But now, at last, I can at least intellectually assimilate all the casts listed above; so the possibilities of the word "expert" may have some potential. Perhaps one day I'll make it.

This would seem a measurable reward after fifty years of trying, but in the final analysis such labels really don't mean anything. I learned this in 1954 when I made the first great cast of my life. The delivery was invented for a particular trout I found one afternoon in a stream in the high desert of western Nevada, while on a deer hunt with my father. The trout was black. She was more than that, she was ebony and onyx, thick and long, like a dark shark at dawn when you are on the flats and can see only the obsidian shape. She carried no spots, or at least none that I could see at first. There was no olive on her shoulders and apparently no rainbow stripe on her sides when she rolled and opened her mouth to take a natural, nor could I detect any silver or pearl. Her pectorals were large and strong, like the wings of a stealth bomber or a dark angel if there are such things, and she floated in the pool like a magician, easily and without regard for the three or four other trout that shared whatever part of the pool she would give them.

The others were much smaller and ordinary, but she was extraordinary and what made her so palpably exciting was the certainty that I was the first to find her. I knew no one had seen her since her cold birth in spring gravel perhaps eight years before; no one had fished for her through the months of drought when no rain would come or through the ice that crystallized above her head in winter.

Fishing for such wild and virginal trout has been defined as the end of the road in an angler's search for the best possible sport, but I was lucky because I started there. At the time, fishing for wild trout also seemed a perfect antidote for the anxieties haunting the soul of a shy, introverted twelve-year-old. For that matter it still does, although I've since learned that fishing really isn't a way for a man to stay young; it's simply a good way to stay connected to that part of you which should always be that way.

The pool inhabited by this dark and magical trout was covered by a shroud of vegetation, including an almost impenetrable umbrella of red manzanita and the weathered limbs of a strange, almost leafless kind of tree whose limbs looked like the arms of a monkey. After my initial sighting, I watched the trout through the brushy tangle for half an hour. She was, at the time, the largest I'd ever encountered, and when I checked the tachometer in my chest it was red-lined at about 15,000.

I couldn't help wondering how she had grown so large in such a small creek, and what would happen if and when I hooked her. But how would I do that? Her position seemed unassailable.

At 3:00 she began to feed. I withdrew to a safe distance and began making adjustments in my tackle. After some testing, four double-ought lead shot proved sufficient and were clamped on the leader, just past the end of the line, and by turning the reel handle backward I was able to make a "split-shot vertical drop cast" in which the line paid out through the guides in a slow descent through the brushy thicket.

Suddenly the trout chased one of her smaller companions into the shallows where it tried to hide. This is interesting, I thought. She's a shark. How did the others survive their first year or two with her? I kept winding backward and the split shot vertical drop cast unfolded until my Coachman fly dangled over the center of the pool.

Perfect, I thought. Maybe I had her. Maybe I would kill her. In 1952, we killed every one we legally could as a matter of moral and lawful right, as a reward for the time, money and energy expended in catching them, but mostly as manifest proof of our tenacity and skill—and, of course, as one way of expanding the dimensions of one's you-know-what.

I could see the fly going down to her and I watched the brown spread of its hackle legs. Maybe, I thought, she'll see it as a spider descending on a filament of silk and wait until it begins to drown before she sucks it in.

She saw the fly and moved toward it, then stopped. "Wait a minute," I could almost hear her saying to herself, "Something is wrong with this thing." Her pupils were focused as she held silently below the fly and studied it and I figured I had all of three seconds to do something before it was all over and I'd lost her forever. "That's all right, honey," I whispered. "It's either this, or the Winchester tomorrow." But I was lying and I knew it. I couldn't kill her. She was too beautiful. Now she was tilting her head, looking hard at the dangling fly, and for the first time I considered the possibility of sentiment in a trout.

It took less than five seconds (I counted) for my tapping on the rod handle to produce the vibrations that ran down the line and leader to the eye of the Coachman's hook, which transformed the motionless fly into a living thing that spread rings of magic across the surface of the pool in a series of ever-enlarging concentric circles. That made her cock her head and come back for a second look. "Hmm," I imagined her saying. "Maybe I was wrong. It couldn't do that unless it was alive, could it?"

"Hell, no," I answered. "For God's sake, just take it."

The sun flashed briefly and suddenly I could see her coming all the way, standing on her tail. She wasn't black at all. She was magenta and purple. The slash of red along her flanks was deeply colored, the linear tattoo of a wine-colored skin that glowed in an amethyst light. There were spots on her back and they looked as large as dimes.

When she returned to her secret pool, my best Apache cry rolled down the stony run of that little creek I'll never see again but will never forget, and as she pulled she had me on the string and I followed, hypnotized by the ring of her rise. And in that second of time, as her tail slipped back through the meniscus, I realized that was the best cast I'd ever made.

I released her not much later in a stream of orange light. The stones beneath her belly were shining and when I looked up at the sky it was full of thunder and lightning. I could smell the coming rain. How often does it rain here? I asked, but she didn't answer. I think she wanted to go home and forget about the whole affair, and just when I thought she'd never forgive me, she spoke. "No hard feelings, pal," she said. "That was one hell of a cast and you got me fair and square."

When she was gone I looked up at the canyon rim and felt a vague yet powerful connection, the impulse of a hunter, I suppose, and imagined those who had been here before me. They appeared in an imaginary line, a long row of human forms standing watch on the edge of the world. They surveyed the landscape below—the river, the rainbow walls of cathedral stone, and the boy whose shaking fingers had just held the wet flanks of what was to him the world's largest trout. One of the figures stepped forward and saluted silently. Then he turned, threw his spear into the sun and disappeared into the clouds.

Many years later, after being well educated (from a perspective consistent with visions of immense trout and salmon; my Comanche brothers on the canyon rim, or whoever they were, and a liberal agenda of parties, political science, evolution, anthropology and the migraine inquiry of statistical analysis), I made the third great cast of my life on the beautifully manicured flats and concrete casting ponds at the Golden Gate Angling and Casting Club in San Francisco, happily entrenched in my chosen profession as a ruined man who loved to fish.

In those days I fished most passionately for steelhead in northern California and sometimes began my casting practice by stretching the monofilament I spliced behind my thirty-foot shooting heads. One day the guy sitting on the bench next to me while I stretched my line wanted to talk about casting. And that was all he wanted to talk about. He went on without stopping for thirty minutes about all the really great casts he had made over the years and how important casting really is in the overall scheme of things.

"It's everything," he said. "It's better than a Ferrari, a membership at Augusta and three nights with Bridget Bardot."

He's really into this, I thought. So I figured he would understand when I told him about that day in Nevada and how I caught a three-pound trout on a creek you could almost straddle, with four split shot and one of the best presentations I'd ever make, without a back cast or forward cast and underneath a tree that looked like a monkey, while a Comanche war party stood watching on the canyon rim.

He smiled and nodded as if he understood, but I could see he didn't. He was a little worried about just what he might have uncovered. I could see it in his eyes.

Then he began talking to someone he apparently had sitting in the back seat of his mind. I was uncertain of her name, but "Poopsie" would be a good guess. I am also uncertain of the exact language he was using but I'm certain it went something like this: "Poopsie," he said, rolling his eyes, "this guy either has one oar out of the water or is suffering from some kind of genetic disability. Look at his hair. Anyone who looks like that or has those kinds of ideas and even thinks he sees those kinds of things couldn't be much of a caster, could he?"

"No, Dearie, he couldn't," Poopsie replied.

But I'll tell you what: Everything changed when I stood up, waved to Poopsie through the windows of this guy's eyes, then turned into the wind, made three double hauls, and launched the next cast—all 120 feet of it—right over the end of the frigging pond.

The Play's the Thing

My Aunt Minnie was no slouch as an angler. She had the best collection of colored cork floats in Warsaw County, Missouri, a tubular steel bait-casting rod, and a reel with the gears of a winch. Forty-pound snelled hooks were a common appliance as were the nine-inch airborne night crawlers that went streaking along for the ride. Now and then she would switch to minnows for crappies (always her favorites) and I felt sorry not only for them, but for the farm-pond bass and bluegill that had the misfortune to meander by one of Minnie's minnows. No quarter was given, none was asked and when the float submerged and she set the hook, vertebrae popped and eyes were crossed by the force of her swing.

It ran in the family. I had an older cousin who was one hell of a baseball player and ended up playing centerfield for the New York Yankees and getting his share of home runs. Now that I think about it, I might have been able to chalk up a few assists by borrowing one of Jerry's gloves and standing behind my aunt when she set the hook, fielding the pop-up crappies and bass she launched to the bleachers behind home plate. But it's too late now.

In retrospect, I realize she was something special, holder of a distinguished chair in a long lineage of dedicated warm-water anglers. She was a Southern Baptist minimalist, the best I've ever fished with.

Watching her was a serious introduction to the art and science of hooking, playing and landing fish in the most efficient manner possible. Along the way I became possessed by the image of her hauling in fish after fish. A certain perspective emerged and eventually grew into a dogma: The more fish you hook and land, the more fun you will have, and the more impressed you'll be with yourself. I'm not sure, for those of us addicted, that such a sentiment ever disappears completely.

But no matter the species or tackle, in my opinion the fault for losing a fish almost always originates in the angler's mind. I know a guy named Pete who runs steelhead trips on some godforsaken part of the planet, Russia I think, and over the years he's had it with guys who end up standing in the middle of the river with a shattered leader yelling, "The sonofabitch broke me off! He broke me off!" For some reason they always repeat the exclamation, Pete says, and it's always a male fish that did the breaking.

"No, it didn't," he replies. "It's the other way around. You broke it off. You put too much pressure on your terminal tackle. And how do you know it was a male?"

My own weaknesses are no less forgivable. My favorite bad habit is to go nuts at exactly the wrong moment. Certain species and situations seem to inspire this more than others. Marlin are the worst because I want them more, having landed fewer than any other fish I've tried for, and also because they can be rather sizable (try 1,000 pounds or more), and because the implications of the hook-up are serious. Marlin lift themselves from the rolling ocean like a Polaris missile with erect pectorals for wings and a neon body of turquoise, silver and hard-edged black. And marlin, especially blue marlin, do not simply take flies and then pull hard. They stab your fly, crush it in their mouth and then suck all the juice out of your body on the first run.

It is an interesting process, a far cry from trout angling in the Beaverkill or Madison. Billfish anglers work in pairs as a team and take turns or "shots," casting to fish that come to investigate the hookless lures trolled behind the boat as "teasers." There are all kinds of theories about teasers, what size and color they should be, how they should swim, how many you should troll, and in what position and how far back from the boat, etc. The selection and pattern of these lures is called "a spread." Like most fishing, the science of billfishing eventually peters out, because no one knows for sure what the fish is thinking, or what it will do next.

If you're lucky, there is a damn good chance that, in a matter of seconds, you will get what you asked for—a hook-up—and everything will go to hell. Veteran anglers rely on experience, mythology, magic, rumors and prayers, and their final selection of the spread is as much an act of faith as anything else. I have seen guys spit on the teasers, rub them across certain parts of their anatomy, then kiss them (the teasers, that is), and three hours later, after several changes of struggling lures have chugged across twenty-five miles of ocean without so much as a gull taking a look, the angler goes to the transom, stares out at the endless sea and gives his best imitation of a Navajo chant. The most optimistic among us urinate while we're singing.

The tackle is absurd. Some sports argue to the contrary, but it's no use. Who are they kidding? It *is* absurd. The reels are capable of winching an army Jeep out of the mud and the rods resemble javelins used in the Olympic games. The lines could truss up a tranquilized grizzly and hold it until the exam was finished. The flies—at least the ones I use—are almost a foot long and strung with a pair of hooks that seem capable of holding a rhino.

Perhaps because of the tackle required, some astute hands seriously denounce the game as "not being fly fishing," but I suspect they started angling with No. 12 Royal Wulffs and never got over it. The essence of billfishing, the best of it, lies in the size, power and violence of the fish, the fantastic suddenness with which they appear and strike the fly in a manner that will rearrange your chromosomes. My advice is not to worry about the gear being too heavy, or too big. It begins to shrink as soon as you connect.

When the angler has decided a pursuing fish is close enough, or when the captain screams NOWGODDAMMITNOW!, the teaser is taken away from the fish and the cast is made to one side and slightly behind the marlin, so it has to turn and take it going away. This gives the angler the best shot at the hook "drawing back" and taking hold in the corner of a very, very hard mouth. By the time the fly is ingested and the balloon of exploding water recedes sufficiently for you to see the horizon again, the fish is streaking off at almost thirty miles an hour. The half-pound javelin rod is now indistinguishable from the "midge" trout rod on page ninety-five of the Orvis catalogue; the reel seems thimble-sized and may be smoking if it cost you less than $500. The line feels like piano wire that will snap at any second, if the twenty-pound tippet doesn't go first.

It's a great play, one every angler should try at least once. And don't argue about the tackle you'll need to land one of these fish.

A case in point: Not long ago a friend and I were fishing at a place called Crocodile Bay Lodge, near the small village of Puerto Jimenez, just outside the Golfito area of southern Costa Rica. Crocodile Bay Lodge has excellent inshore and offshore fishing for a multitude of species—from roosterfish, jack crevalle and snook inshore to tuna, wahoo and dorado offshore—but Lou and I were chasing billfish. Mostly sails.

On the third day, four blue marlin were landed by other boats fishing north of our beat. Our captain and mate were obviously excited and asked if Lou and I would like to change our bearings and give it a shot. They added that they wanted fresh everything for the next day: new leaders, lines, flies and hooks, and told us to be sure to check all our knots. Every one.

That night, during the re-rigging, the tension began to build. Until that time I had hooked five blue marlin on a fly and lost them all. Each weighed more than 200 pounds. I have taken two on conventional gear, one just at 200 pounds and the other of medium size (in marlin lingo), weighing close to 380. But I don't think that's enough to qualify as sufficient experience; so I began to get very "nervioso."

At 10:00 the next morning we were almost forty miles offshore. There was just a slight breeze and the sea was nearly flat. The water was something between cobalt and some shade for which there seems no name, and we trolled smoothly along a seam of current and foam that indicated God knows what, but which I hoped represented some kind of feeding lane. Perfect.

At 10:45 a nearby boat, the *Nitembe*, suddenly hooked a blue on conventional tackle and we watched as the fish literally split the ocean apart with a series of spectacular jumps, ripping some 200 yards of line from the angler's reel in a matter of seconds as it went greyhounding across the surface. It may seem like a stretch to compare the sight of that fish with images I've seen of the Space Shuttle, but in fact the resemblance was truthful. It was spectacular.

I could feel my pulse quickening as Lou watched, turned to me and said, "Listen, Waller, there's no way, man. There's no fucking way you could land one of those on a fly rod. Any kind of fly rod. If we raise one, it's yours. I don't want it. I want you to take the shot. I know how badly you want one."

Now I've fished with Lou long enough to know he doesn't frighten easily, but I swear that what I heard in his voice then was indeed fear, or at least high-modulus anxiety. And for good reason, I thought. This is serious stuff.

I considered his offer. "No way, Jose," I finally replied. "It's a doable deal, Lou. It can be done. I know a few guys who have done it. If a blue comes to the teasers and you're up, it's your shot. I won't take your shot."

Our mate, Scott Stinson, joined us in watching the *Nitembe's* runaway blue, then turned to the sea, made a gesture of homage and good luck, zipped up, and began setting the spread of teasers. Meanwhile I watched the angler in the other boat as his rod bent almost double, a graphite semicircle pointing down to some interminable point far below the surface. Now he's in for it, I thought. The fish had sounded.

Scott turned to Lou and raised his eyebrows but said nothing. The spread was set and I watched as my fishing partner stepped up to the plate and coiled his line on the deck with the fly and leader on the transom and the rod down next to the gunwale with the tip pointing to a cloudy horizon.

Then something unusual happened. Eduardo, our captain, changed places with Scott. "For good luck," Eduardo said. Scott usually captains another boat but had volunteered to do first-mate duties this day. He wanted to be there if it happened.

A half hour passed. Then another forty-five minutes. The radio crackled again and Scott took the call. "They got the blue," he said. "I know the *Nitembe's* captain. He's a friend, a guy named Mike. We surf and fish together. He says the fish will go 300 pounds, maybe more. That's five blue marlin we've found out here in two days, including the 650-pounder the kid got with me two days ago. You guys be ready, goddammit. They're here."

I could feel the adrenalin rising; boundaries of common sense begin to fade and it all began to take on the feel of some kind of very bizarre, surreal drama. I could feel myself fighting to stay calm. I was zero for five and the last one I saw was a real smoker that took the popper by leaping fifteen feet across the surface, five feet in the air, and snarfing the twelve-inch fly on the way back in. "Over 250," the captain told us. The marlin tail wrapped the line on the strike and when the line broke it sounded like a gunshot.

That's all right, I said to myself. Just pretend it's a sailfish if it comes when you're up. You can do it.

Now it was 2:00. The unknown angler on the *Nitembe* had hooked a second blue and again we could see it jumping. Scott turned twenty degrees to the south and repeated his admonition: "You guys stay ready. It's going to happen."

When I thought about it, this all seemed so serious, so oddly distorted. Maybe Hemingway was right: maybe these fish are really birds. The *Nitembe's* marlin was flying like one, crashing back and forth, sailing through the sky as the angler yielded line. It was easily as large as the one landed earlier. Lou and I watched, spellbound. I started to reach for a couple of beers.

"Hey, you fuggers," Scott whispered. "I said be ready."

It was one of those dream-like moments when the emotional needle goes from zero to red-line in two seconds. Everything happened in slow motion; yet it was moving at the speed of light. All I know is that Eduardo, maybe Scott and probably everyone else, including me, screamed "Marlin! Marlin! Marlin!" over and over again until I cleared the inactive teaser, Scott had drawn up the outrigger lures and Eduardo had teased the fish to no more than fifteen feet from the transom.

I never saw Lou's cast. When I looked his shoulders were rolled forward and he looked like a fighter about to land a left hook as he stripped in the fly. Then the ocean erupted in front of him, split open by the size of the fish.

David and Goliath, I thought. I could see her immense body, black and ominous, rolling in the white lace of foam and propwash, cutting through it, back and forth like a shark, looking for the fly and slashing for it.

Then she took. I could see the light in her eye, and how amazingly silver and blue she looked as she raised herself effortlessly from the surface and past the horizon; for a moment she seemed frozen as she held the fly in her bill, then she climbed to an impossible height before she crashed again and went screaming away.

She seemed some kind of strange, beautiful creature—only half fish, the rest of her some kind of beast of the sea, with a coat of steel, blue wings and tail, running at breathtaking speed. Other fish may be at home in the water, but a marlin is the only species I have seen that seems to dominate the sea itself. She was indeed something to reckon with, and something to fear. I thought of the incident near Mazatlan some years ago when a blue ran its bill through the mate, somehow not killing him but fatally injuring the angler who stood behind him. Sonofabitch! I thought. Lou has her on. Sonofabitch!

The next thing I knew Lou was shouting, "I'm running out of line. I'm running out of line. Somebody do something." I looked at his reel but couldn't see the handle. The spool was a blur but I could see how much backing was left and wished I hadn't been the one to tie it to the arbor of the reel. But there was nothing I could do about that now, nothing anyone could do but hang in there and try to follow the fish. I was reminded that unless you were Aunt Minnie, there were always three acts to the play—and the first one was just getting started.

Act one always belongs to the fish—trout, bass or marlin. The angler's posture is defensive. They act. You react. The second act is anyone's guess. Take the advantage when you can; yield when you must. Then the third act begins and things reverse: You act, they react. If you're patient, if you're lucky, and if you do not exceed the limits of your terminal gear, you win.

There are ways to practice this, but few take the time. It's as simple as tying your fly to some object and pulling over and over again until you know exactly how much pressure it will take to break your leader. Memorize the tension in your fingers, hand and arm, and never exceed those boundaries. After a while a "pattern of sensation" will emerge and then you'll have the feel. It's called knowing the limits of your tackle and never exceeding them no matter what act of the play you are in.

It's also important to become familiar with your reel's drag, if it has one. Some drags tighten in one direction, others in the opposite. Knowledge of this has to be automatic so that you don't have to stop during the heat of the battle and think about which way to turn the knob.

But sometimes, no matter how well prepared you are, the hook just pulls out. So it was with Lou's fish. After an hour and a half, two trips deep under the boat and countless runs—half of them in the air, or so it seemed—she finally decided to see what would happen if she ran straight at us. Before Lou or Scott could do anything about it, she was off.

She would have been, as far as I know, one of the largest blue marlin ever landed on a fly. Maybe the largest.

Lou had done everything right.

"Where in the hell did that guy learn to play a fish?" Scott wanted to know. "He was as cool as a cucumber."

"Fuck if I know," I said. "I probably taught him everything he knows."

"OK," someone asked, "How big was it?"

"Well, it was a female," Scott replied. "Actually one of the smallest I've hooked here. But she was big enough. She would have beaten the record by a bunch. I'd give her an honest 325 pounds, maybe 350. Man, I really wanted her. I'm zero for eight on the fly now, and we were so damn close. I thought Eduardo had her about halfway through the fight when she drifted close to the boat. He had the gloves on. Did you see the leader? She was only ten feet away. God, it was close."

There are moments that can change an angler's life. I looked at Lou and thought maybe this was one of those moments for him. He looked funny—happy and sad at the same time—and more than a little drained. His eyes were shining.

"You were right," he told me. "The lady in the blue suit. Shit. What a deal that is. I want to do this again. As soon as possible. Did you see that thing?"

It had happened. I had just watched a guy go over the edge and return, wanting more. And more. Always more.

I remembered a time two years ago at Billy Pate's tournament in Quepos. It was raining like hell and the mud in the street ran like freshly poured cement and the wind was howling, but it didn't' matter; the sails were running good. I was sitting with my partner, Steve Myers, and Jimmy Gallagher and his partner, Jeffrey, were there too.

Jeffrey had just taken a blue of more than 200 pounds and was explaining about how you had to do that kind of thing to really know what it means to be alive.

He ran down his calendar for us: ten months of billfishing all over the world, in Costa Rica, Panama, Venezuela, Australia and Mexico, then back again. "Goddamn," he said. "I love it. It's all I want do. I've been doing it for twelve years now, almost non-stop."

"You married?" I asked him.

"Not any more," he said.

I thought of Jim Gray's video we had watched earlier. Spent and exhausted after several hours of playing and finally landing his world-record blue, Gray was lying on deck next to the dead fish. His face was white and the muscles in his back had gone into spasms. Gray's shirt seemed tattooed on his body. Blood ran on the deck mixed with salt water and sweat and it looked like he was crying. I wouldn't blame him if he was. The blue weighed 260 pounds.

I thought of my friend Les Eichorn's day-long fight with a world-record black marlin in Australia waters, which ended just as the mate reached for the nylon and the hooks pulled free and the marlin disappeared. Les said that in a way it didn't matter, because things had gotten to the point that he knew what the fish would do next, and somehow that seemed enough.

I thought of my own four-hour battle with a Pacific sailfish, of all the trout, steelhead, bass, crappie, tarpon, bonefish and permit I'd struggled with, even the monstrous seventeen-pound carp I once hooked on a No. 14 Hare's Ear Nymph, and all the rest—those I got, and those I didn't get but still remember after all these years. And I knew I'd be ready for my next marlin shot.

No, I don't know if I can pull it off. But I can try, and besides, in the end it doesn't matter how big or small they are, or even if you get them or not. Because the play's the thing.

Sockeye Messengers (for Bill Allan)

The salmon were cleanly focused, magnified by the clarity of the water and my own admiration for them. Pushing hard upstream, only a few feet away, they brought to mind a fleet of phantom ships returning home with tattooed fins for sails and rudders and a compass in their hearts or brains. One particularly ragged male had the quick, searching head of a wolf.

The school was smooth and soundless. Their salmon eyes burned brightly and I could see them scanning the boulders and gravel like radar. But most seemed to be in trouble; their bodies were rotting away so rapidly it looked as if they would disintegrate long before the salmon could reach their spawning grounds. I felt sorry for them and wondered if they were in pain. "They are more than ships," I thought. "They are great warriors." The odyssey was magnificent, timeless.

Moments such as these seem essential and as inescapable as a bad cast, and as the salmon passed in perfect single file, my thoughts turned to a longtime friend, West Coast angler and artist Bill Allan, who taught me a great deal about how to see salmon. During the late 1970s we photographed a declining run of coho salmon and wild steelhead in northern California's Papermill Creek, material for a series of watercolors Bill was doing at the time.

Papermill is an almost completely urban proposition. The fish there have to roll over and give up their milt and eggs to gravel that in places may be less than 100 feet from a highway. The asphalt carries weekend tourists on their way to the Point Reyes coast for steaming barbecued oysters, plus a relatively few locals (compared to San Francisco forty miles away) and some teenagers who hook-shoot their beer cans over the car tops into the pools and riffles of the creek.

That's not all. Now and then the Lone Ranger and Tonto leave their hot tubs and corrals in the nearby town of Woodacre and take their horses on an exercising gallop up the creek and through the salmon redds, scattering terrified female coho that refuse to abort their buried eggs as they try to hide in water scarcely deep enough to cover their ripened flanks. A few of the weaker ones eventually will be pitch-forked or stoned to death. I have often thought that upper Papermill Creek may be one of the few spawning rivers more difficult for salmon and steelhead to ascend than the gauntlet of concrete and steel dams along the Columbia River and its tributaries.

Bill and I have hoped the salmon's true nature could someday penetrate at least some part of the collective consciousness of urban America and simultaneously remind some of us why we like to go fishing, but that hasn't happened yet and there doesn't appear to be much hope that it will. Some days I'm not certain of the future and fear we may yet end up finally breaking the genetic chain of purely wild salmon. I remember Tom Brokaw's newscast several seasons ago in which he reported on the number of wild sockeye salmon that had returned successfully to their native spawning grounds in the upper Columbia drainage. The number was one.

I'm less confused about why I'm out there and the reasons are personal. I have boundless respect for those few salmon that remain and cannot bring myself to step on them when they are dead and I'm fishing through their pool. Bill was right: They are true warriors, living like ghosts in an age that seems neither to see them nor honor them. Yet the salmon refuse to surrender or stop doing their best, and that's more than you can say for many of us who fish for them.

It's a pessimist's dream come true: We could set more of the salmon spawning riffles off limits to the incompatible elements of civilization, but most likely we will not. Our riparian philosophy fits nicely into the needs of a growing population; pollution threatens to choke our cities and most of our coastal rivers are blocked by dams. One could argue that the python has finally found its own throat.

And yet, the salmon—all five Pacific species—have always returned innocently for more. For millennia they have been the perfect masters of all our West Coast waters. I can never fish for them without wondering what they have to say. What are they trying to tell us? What message do they bring? Those questions bring to mind a line from Russell Chatham's book *The Angler's Coast*, which, as I recall, goes something like this: "To crack the salmon would be to crack the universe."

The pull of a steelhead comes suddenly, with a tug that springs up the line and brings the rod to life in sharp, tensile excitement, ending my reverie of Bill Allan paintings and the wolf-headed ghosts of electricity I see in the burning eyes of salmon. For just a moment I look away from the sockeye and try to find a sign of my spooling fish. Then, as the darting hen stalls in a deep tongue of current, a red leaf of October drops tantalizingly past the corner of my eye, almost out of reach. Old habits die hard; I grab for it, still fielding pop-ups at sixty-one years of age.

From my point of view it is enjoyable chaos: baseball, falling leaves and runaway steelhead merge naturally with clean water, forests still untouched by chainsaws and frogs that can talk, including one that has watched me with a wary eye as I shuffled around in its territory. It is all a powerful reminder of our humble place in the grand scheme of things and the magic one can find there, including the seasons which in part define our lives as anglers. All you have to do is turn your cell phone off and start looking and listening.

Anadromous fish seem especially prophetic. Their life cycles make it so and as the hen steelhead slows, shakes her head and burrows into dark water, I feel a portent of winter snows and cold, frozen rivers. When she turns and runs again, everything heats up; spring and summer break loose in the green cottonwood and aspen buds that surround her spawning pool. And when her shoulders break the surface in a final corkscrew roll, I can imagine her impossible, fantastic return to the river and the skein of eggs deep inside her body. All pass in an endless circle, magnified and revealed, and I haven't aged one second. If anything, I'm going in the opposite direction. This isn't bad, I think. My e-mail can go to hell.

And perhaps that's another part of the message. Maybe fishing is just another way of staying young forever—but before I can pull the chain and win the dough for knowing all the right answers, the fish is gone, having pulled free from the hook. The red leaf drops from my hand into a waning light, finds another breeze and in my imagination metamorphoses into a moth. As it strikes the surface, it scurries upriver in the dark wind, holding its skirt, chasing after the salmon. Everything goes around the corner and disappears into the thickening night.

I think it may be time to quit, even though a second steelhead rolls dimly in the tail of the pool followed momentarily by a third. My reason for stopping is also personal: It has been many years since I have had any interest in beaching a steelhead whose colors and form I could not see. What's the point? Allan's paintings and my own values put an end to all of that.

"So wind it up, my good man," the red-eyed frog says, "and go back to camp—and next time check the hook before you cast."

Each spooling click of the Hardy reel is a second, then a minute, then a day and a week, then a month, and suddenly and quite amazingly, it has been two years and I'm in Alaska, this time chasing silver salmon, tromping up and down a brackish estuary somewhere on the spongy tundra and mud flats of Bristol Bay with long-time angling companions Richard Evans and Carl Engel. The tin-colored old Hardy Perfect with the worn-out white handle clicks loudly again as I strip line and draw the rod back for another one of Geronimo's arrow-straight casts. Maybe.

The salmon here on Amakadori creek are fresh, stapled with sea lice, strong and silver, riding on the wind and crashing waves, and just as I launch my first cast into a tidal pool filled with triangular wakes and silver dorsals, I remember what Henry Thoreau said: "Some men fish their entire lives without knowing it is not fish they are after." Well, if it isn't fish, then what the hell is it?

Take your choice. Here's mine: Much of what I'm looking for isn't recreation, and has little to do with fish, although they are the perfect reminders. What I am looking for is a connection. The Connection.

The tide is flooding and the salmon are agitated. If it's going to happen, I think, it's going to happen now. The wind eases up and I finally get in a good cast. Geronimo's arrow slices through the surface, dragging a No. 8 blue Comet, my leader, Henry Thoreau and everything else down with it. Despite the tidal surge, the line's compound swing is slow and close to a 45-degree angle. At the count of five the eye of a salmon sees the fly coming in the arctic light. At seven the salmon is breathing on it. At eight he takes. The hook is set and the connection is made. I am the conduit. Some strange euphoria runs up the line, passes through the old reliable carpal tunnel system and connects me to the stones on which I stand.

When I look down at them I don't see a lot of money, as so many people do. I see instead the simple markers of my life as a fisherman, and the choice seems well made. After the third or fourth jump, just after the howling reel is wrenched from the sliding bands on the reel seat of the rod, my own journey and that of all fishermen who care about this kind of stuff seems no less magical or honest than that of the salmon and trout we pursue, or the rivers which carry them. The connection is complete and for the moment there is no other place on earth I would rather be.

The mouth of a salmon is beautifully dark; this one is yawning for oxygen as he comes to shore with the comet still burning in the hinge of his jaw, and I imagine his panic as he tries to utilize an atmosphere that is suffocating him. An apology would seem in order for this and for all the dams, the poison in his water, the clear-cutting of his forests, and the great holes we are making in his sky. I make it as his eyes focus downward and his stomach touches the pure ripple of Amakadori creek, and no matter how many times I have one in my grip, I will always wonder what they really think as I feel them slipping away forever, lost in rivers that I fear are running out of both water and time.

"You are a fool if you don't tell them," the salmon says as he glides away into the closing blanket. I know he's right. The connection is not recreational; it is necessary. Our own lives are enriched for having known the salmon and we cannot afford to lose them, or their rivers. If we do, we will lose some irreplaceable part of ourselves. And it is more than that. In the end all human enterprise, development, growth and well being is dependent on the earth and the water it holds. It is not magical animism. It is the truth: Our Salmon are talking and so are the trees, each and every animal, each breath of air, our shadows and all our rivers.

I've thought about that for some time now, during good casts and bad, and through long winters when there was no fishing at all, and if it sounds naive, or beside the point, you might consider the possibility that you picked up this book by mistake.